MEGA

Mild/Moderate Cross Categorical Special Education Practice Questions

I0866801

Mometrix

TEST PREPARATION

Dear Future Exam Success Story

First of all, **THANK YOU** for purchasing Mometrix study materials!

Second, congratulations! You are one of the few determined test-takers who are committed to doing whatever it takes to excel on your exam. **You have come to the right place.** We developed these practice tests with one goal in mind: to deliver you the best possible approximation of the questions you will see on test day.

Standardized testing is one of the biggest obstacles on your road to success, which only increases the importance of doing well in the high-pressure, high-stakes environment of test day. Your results on this test could have a significant impact on your future, and these practice tests will give you the repetitions you need to build your familiarity and confidence with the test content and format to help you achieve your full potential on test day.

Your success is our success

We would love to hear from you! If you would like to share the story of your exam success or if you have any questions or comments in regard to our products, please contact us at **800-673-8175** or **support@mometrix.com**.

Thanks again for your business and we wish you continued success!

Sincerely,
The Mometrix Test Preparation Team

Table of Contents

Practice Test #1

1. Javier is a third-grade student who just moved from Mexico and is struggling with the content in his English class. Which of the following is the best reason for not evaluating him for special education services right away?

a. Students who are English learners are not eligible for special education services.
b. It is best to wait and see which disability he may have.
c. It is best to wait and see the nature of his struggles.
d. New students often take a while to learn a new curriculum.

2. Which of the following best describes the purpose of state standardized tests?

a. To compare a student's academic achievement to a norm
b. To determine how much progress a student has made
c. To find strengths and weaknesses in a student's development
d. To determine the intellectual ability of students

3. Which of the following is most important in writing nondiscriminatory assessments?

a. Getting to know the background of each student in the class
b. Ensuring the inclusion of multicultural questions
c. Eliminating biases associated with certain topics
d. Evaluating each student based on their identity

4. Brian is a 12th-grade student with an intellectual disability. Which of the following would be the best example of a functional curriculum in his science class?

a. Learning how to conduct an experiment
b. Learning how to read a book about planets
c. Learning how to maintain a garden
d. Learning how to calculate speed

5. Dustin is a ninth-grade student who struggles with his organizational skills. Which of the following assistive technology devices would be most beneficial in helping him improve these skills?

a. FM listening systems
b. Speech recognition programs
c. Data managers
d. Abbreviation expanders

6. Trevor is a fifth-grade student with co-occurring conditions as a student with a specific learning disability and an emotional disturbance. Which of the following is a benefit of identifying Trevor in both of these areas?

a. Trevor can receive academic and emotional support.
b. Trevor can be placed in a self-contained classroom.
c. Trevor can have a behavior plan.
d. Trevor can be eligible for alternative placement.

7. Which of the following is most accurate about what teachers need to consider in planning lessons in reading and math for both special needs students and the class as a whole?

a. They already know which skill or concept they want to teach.
b. They assume students have prerequisites for a skill/concept.
c. They must determine what mastery of a skill/concept requires.
d. They are premature in thinking how to expand/apply learning.

8. A student was referred for a complete evaluation to determine eligibility for Special Education Services. Tests yield levels of cognitive and adaptive functioning. Which of the following is correct about how these results may be used?

a. They may be used in describing the student's present level of functioning on the student's IEP.
b. They may be used as baselines to compare later scores in assessing program effectiveness.
c. They may be used to determine the student's levels for placement in Special Education services.
d. They may be used to make a medical diagnosis, such as Autism Spectrum Disorder.

9. Clyde is 16 years old, has visual impairment, and reads on a first-grade level. What would be a good choice of materials for his teacher to provide him?

a. Large-print books on subjects relevant to teens
b. Children's books, which have large print and simple text
c. Regular library books with a magnifying glass
d. Large-print books with subjects geared to teens but with simplified text

10. Which of the following would be the LEAST productive method for determining how a test at the end of the unit can be used to improve instruction for the next unit?

a. Identifying which questions the students struggled with
b. Identifying which students struggled on the test
c. Identifying which kinds of questions the students asked
d. Identifying which curriculum to use

11. George is a sixth-grade student with a specific learning disability in the area of written expression. Which of the following assistive technology devices would likely be LEAST beneficial to George?

a. Graphic organizers
b. Proofreading programs
c. Frequency modulation (FM) listening systems
d. Word-prediction programs

12. Joseph is a fourth grader who receives special education services as a student with an other health impairment due to his attention deficit hyperactivity disorder. Which formative assessment would be MOST appropriate when starting a new lesson?

a. Giving him a math test to complete at the end of the unit
b. Giving him a fact test to complete before the unit
c. Monitoring his progress throughout the unit
d. Monitoring his behavior during the test

13. In teaching basic mathematics, the following actions by teachers will benefit all students. However, which one is most likely to be needed more specifically for students with special needs in a general education classroom?

a. Carefully planning the coverage and order of instructional math content
b. Judicious selection and application of the specific instructional strategies
c. Designing practice activities that take a wide range of student needs into account
d. Giving intensive, direct instruction in mathematics to individual students

14. Which of these is a recommended teaching strategy for students with dyscalculia?

a. Students should be discouraged from using estimates to begin solving math problems.
b. Teachers should present new material by moving from abstract to concrete examples.
c. Teachers should offer alternative explanations for math facts instead of rote learning.
d. Students should not have to use graph paper if they have trouble organizing on paper.

15. Why are objectives important for lesson planning when teaching a group of students with deficits in executive functioning?

a. To provide students the opportunity to plan what they will be learning
b. To assess students at the end of the lecture
c. To give students a task to complete during their learning
d. To keep students focused on one learning goal

16. A ninth-grade student with a learning disability in the area of reading can read words with high accuracy but has difficulty understanding what she reads. Which of the following components is the most important to focus on?

a. Fluency
b. Vocabulary
c. Phonics
d. Comprehension

17. Which of the following is true regarding individuals with developmental disabilities today?

a. Their life expectancies have not increased in the way those of nondisabled people have.
b. The majority of funding for developmental disabilities is allocated for family support.
c. Mandated school services have increased expectations of support for aging at home.
d. Adults with developmental disabilities are not at higher risk for chronic health issues.

18. Freddy is a sixth-grade student who is struggling with his math class. Freddy's math teacher has provided some remediation to his work, but he is still struggling. What would be the MOST appropriate next step?

a. Evaluate Freddy for special education.
b. Continue providing remediation.
c. Attempt more intensive interventions.
d. Remove the remediation and collect data.

19. When writing learning objectives, the acronym "SMART" is often used. What do the letters in "SMART" stand for?

a. Systematic, measurable, attainable, reasonable, targeted
b. Specific, measurable, attainable, relevant, time-bound
c. Systematic, measurable, attainable, reasonable, tested
d. Specific, measurable, attainable, reasonable, time-bound

20. Which of the following models used in planning instruction for students with disabilities is described as an example of "student-directed planning"?

a. The model and process of Group Action Planning (GAP)
b. The Choosing Options and Accommodations for Children (COACH) model
c. The model and process of Making Action Plans (MAPs)
d. The Planning Alternative Tomorrows with Hope (PATH) model

21. Which of the following would be the best example of a learning objective that is appropriately challenging for a third-grade student with a disability in reading fluency?

a. The student will be able to identify 25 letters in one minute.
b. The student will be able to identify 25 letter sounds in one minute.
c. The student will be able to read 50 sight words in one minute.
d. The student will be able to read 100 words in one minute.

22. What is NOT typically a responsibility of the special education teacher?

a. Managing paraprofessionals
b. Scheduling Individualized Education Program (IEP) meetings
c. Developing student class schedules
d. Supporting general education teachers

23. Pat is a second-grade student who has been receiving intervention support outside of his general education class for the last six weeks due to difficulties with reading fluency. What steps should the school take if Pat struggles to make progress?

a. Continue interventions for another six weeks.
b. Discontinue interventions.
c. Refer Pat for special education services.
d. Refer Pat for a 504 plan.

24. Anna is a fourth-grade student with a disability who is struggling with reading comprehension in her social studies class. Which of the following would be the best option for ensuring that Anna can appropriately access the general education curriculum?

a. Moving Anna to the third-grade social studies class
b. Reteaching the concepts in her special education class
c. Placing a paraprofessional in her social studies class
d. Modifying the content in her social studies class

25. Which of the following strategies is most effective in measuring the goals of students with behavior concerns?

a. Using curriculum-based measures
b. Comparing students to their peers
c. Counting the number of referrals
d. Using random time samples

26. Which of the following is the most appropriate example of a student with a disability receiving support from a peer tutor on a subject they are struggling with?

a. A 2nd-grade student tutoring a 1st-grade student in math
b. A 12th-grade student tutoring a kindergarten student in reading
c. A 7th-grade student tutoring an 8th-grade student in science
d. An 11th-grade student tutoring a 9th-grade student in writing

27. Adaptive behavior scales are assessments that are often used for students diagnosed with intellectual disabilities. Which area would not typically be assessed in one of these scales?

a. Cognition
b. Communication
c. Motor skills
d. Social skills

28. Lee's scoliosis is so severe that the OT in his residential facility had to build him a flatbed reclining wheelchair, but it is too wide to fit through the behavior specialists' office door for IQ testing. Which is the best alternative location for testing?

a. The hallway outside Lee's classroom
b. Lee's living area upstairs in the facility
c. The inner hallway outside the office
d. Inside Lee's classroom off in a corner

29. To ascertain a student's current achievement status in reading, math, and other subjects, which kinds of instruments are used?

a. Cognitive test instruments
b. A sociocultural evaluation
c. Behavioral observations
d. Educational testing tools

30. Edgar is a seventh-grade student with an other health impairment (OHI) who is new to your caseload. Which strategy would be MOST effective in reducing potential bias toward him?

a. Reviewing his Individualized Education Program (IEP) to ensure his needs are understood
b. Meeting with him to know more about his background
c. Calling his parents to introduce yourself
d. Reviewing his educational record from his previous school

31. For students who are deaf from birth and use sign language, which of the following would an advocate of inclusion NOT consider an inclusive educational strategy?

a. Students attend a general education school and are pulled out for special instruction.
b. Students attend a regional or magnet school whose location requires living apart from their families.
c. All students and teachers in the general education school are taught to use sign language.
d. All classrooms having deaf students are assigned sign language interpreters.

32. Which of the following best describes a developmental assessment?

a. A norm-referenced scale
b. A quick identifier
c. A behavior rating scale
d. An alternate assessment

33. What statement is true regarding literacy?

a. The same literacy skills in students apply across subjects
b. The literacy demands of society have changed over time
c. Literacy required of pupils stays constant across grades
d. Literacy is best taught in the schools in a separate lesson

34. Cory is a 10th-grade student with an OHI due to attention-deficit/hyperactivity disorder. Which one of the following social influences is likely to have the most impact on his academic performance?

a. The education levels of his parents
b. The composition of his household
c. His race or ethnic background
d. The friends he spends time with

35. What strategy listed here is most designed to promote generalization of learning?

a. Having a student practice a new skill in a variety of different settings/contexts
b. Having a student practice a new skill regularly and periodically testing that skill
c. Having a student practice a complex skill one step at a time, and then adding steps
d. Having a student practice a new skill in class before applying it in real-life tasks

36. Ms. Case is planning field trips in the spring for some of her high school classes. One of her groups includes Sarah, who has a diagnosis of severe autism. Which of these would be a suitable activity?

a. A trip to a local Renaissance festival
b. A nature hike to examine local flora
c. A community mixer for her age group
d. An outing to attend a rock concert

37. Matthew is a third-grade student with an emotional disturbance who struggles with outbursts. Which of the following observation methods would be most beneficial when conducting a formative assessment?

a. Tally marks
b. Time sampling
c. Qualitative observations
d. Verbatim scripting

38. Which of the following is true of the extended school year services section of the IEP?

a. All students with IEPs receive extended school year services.
b. Extended school year services must be provided at the beginning of the summer.
c. Extended school year services must be provided before the school year starts.
d. Some students are not eligible for extended school year services.

39. Which of the following is true of the "multiple disabilities" category?

a. Deaf-blindness can be included in the multiple disabilities category.
b. Orthopedic impairments cannot be included in the multiple disabilities category.
c. Students with multiple disabilities cannot be accommodated solely for one impairment.
d. Students with multiple disabilities remain in this category throughout their schooling.

40. An intellectually disabled teen has been offered a job by an elderly neighbor. The neighbor wants the teen to work alongside her in the garden twice a week. They will plant seeds, transplant larger plants, weed, lay mulch, water, and fertilize. Later in the season, they will cut flowers and arrange bouquets, pick produce, and sell it all at the neighbor's roadside stand. The neighbor, the teen's mother, and the teen's special education teacher meet to discuss the proposal. The plan is:

a. Tentatively accepted. Because the teen is excited about having a job, her mother and teacher reluctantly agree. They both know the girl is likely to lose interest quickly, and they caution the neighbor that if she truly needs help, she may want to look elsewhere. However, no one wants to disappoint the girl, and they all decide the experience will be good for her.
b. Rejected. Despite the teen's insistence she can manage these tasks, her mother and teacher believe she cannot. They fear trying will set her up for failure.
c. Rejected. The teacher and her mother are very uncomfortable with the neighbor's offer. They suspect the elderly woman is simply lonely or may be a predator who has selected an intellectually disabled victim because such children are particularly vulnerable.
d. Enthusiastically accepted. The adults discuss a background check and the possibility the teen might discover gardening is not for her and want to quit. However, this is most likely to happen early in her employment, giving the neighbor sufficient time to find another helper.

41. Which of the following is most likely to be true about students with learning disabilities and their families?

a. Families that have children with disabilities typically bond closer.
b. Parents can sometimes be the cause of a learning disability.
c. Parents will often suspect a disability before the school does.
d. Families often seek out information about disabilities.

42. Which of the following health problems is included in the "other health impairment" disability category?

a. Asthma
b. Cerebral palsy
c. Traumatic brain injury
d. Perceptual disability

Refer to the following for question 43:

Mrs. Minor is working on social skills with her high-school-level autism spectrum disorder class. Her students are all high functioning. They do not have difficulty being in crowded or noisy places. They are not averse to being around other people. Their needs involve learning appropriate behaviors in social interactions, initiating social interaction with others, and participating more fully in social activities. She is designing curricula to incorporate social skills across settings.

43. Which of the following strategies can be implemented to best promote a meaningful learning experience for these students?

a. Offering to help each student outside of class
b. Getting to know each student in class
c. Creating experiences on topics that students are interested in
d. Giving rewards for students with high grades

44. Which of these is not an example of assistive technology (AT) that could be used in assessment?

a. A pencil wrapped with tape
b. A text-to-speech computer
c. A word processing program
d. These are all examples of AT

45. Kayla is a fifth-grade student with a specific learning disability in the area of math problem solving. At Kayla's annual IEP meeting, which of the following individuals is required by law to be a member of the IEP team?

a. A school counselor
b. A general education teacher
c. A school psychologist
d. A school social worker

Refer to the following for question 46:

One of Mr. Petrov's high school students struggles significantly with reading comprehension skills. She loses her place often and misreads key words. She doesn't try to correct her errors, even when they make no sense. She can give only a rudimentary summary of what she has read. Based on his observations, Mr. Petrov suspects this student may have a learning disability that requires special education services.

46. Which type of instructional focus would be most beneficial to improve her reading comprehension?

a. Well-organized coaching in decoding, sight words, vocabulary, and comprehension several times a week
b. Weekly instruction on one area of reading; more, and the student will become overwhelmed and likely shut down
c. Instruction aimed at helping her become self-motivated and disciplined in her approach to learning
d. Strategies to help her understand the general meaning so that she can gather context clues

47. Ms. Lewis has a resource room with students who have a variety of different disabilities. One student, Jonathan, has a very slow response time to any stimulus. Another student, Michelle, can work very quickly but needs help focusing her attention. Corey and Jennifer work at a similar pace but are using very different instructional materials. Ms. Lewis has one teacher's aide in her room. Which is the most efficient use of instructional time in this setting?

a. Ms. Lewis works with Jonathan for the first half of the period while the teacher's aide rotates among the other students, then Ms. Lewis works with each of the others for the second half of the period.
b. Ms. Lewis gives Jonathan a stimulus and lets him process it while the aide monitors him and Ms. Lewis then attends to each other student in turn, giving all students equal time.
c. Ms. Lewis works with Corey and Jennifer, since they work at a similar pace, while the aide goes between Jonathan and Michelle.
d. Ms. Lewis concentrates on helping Michelle to focus while the aide goes between the other students.

48. Teddy's family has just moved from an isolated rural area. Teddy has never been taught reading, writing, or arithmetic. According to US federal law, which of the following is true?

a. Teddy may be determined to be functionally disabled.
b. Teddy cannot be judged as disabled only by illiteracy.
c. Teddy cannot receive remedial education for literacy.
d. Teddy's situation is not well covered by federal laws.

49. Which statement is most accurate regarding the Cross-Battery Assessment (XBA) approach?

a. It is an approach to testing for reading and writing disorders that is not evidence-based.
b. It is an approach to testing students across different domains of academic achievement.
c. It is an approach to testing students across different domains of intellectual competence.
d. It is an approach to testing that can enhance comprehensiveness, selectivity, and depth.

50. Which of the following classroom climate factors is most important when working with at-risk learners with disabilities?

a. Allowing the students to access accommodations
b. Providing a caring classroom setting
c. Allowing these students to collaborate with peers
d. Providing opportunities for after-school activities

51. Which of the following is NOT a way to teach children phonological awareness?

a. The jump-rope game "A my name is Alice and I live in Alabama and I sell Apples; B my name is Betty and I live in Boston and I sell Buttons...."
b. Playing the "I Spy" game while shopping, first looking for an "A" in the surroundings, then for a "B," etc., going through the alphabet
c. Singing "The Name Game" song "Shirley, Shirley, Bo birley, Banana fanna fo Firley, Fee fie mo Mirley, Shirley!" etc.
d. Reading Dr. Seuss books to and with children (e.g., Green Eggs and Ham, The Foot Book, Great Day for Up)

52. Jessica is a fourth-grade student with a specific learning disability in the area of reading comprehension. How might technology be incorporated into a reading lesson plan in order to meet her needs?

a. Allowing her to research a story on the computer
b. Allowing her to access audiobooks
c. Allowing her to give a presentation instead of a reading
d. Allowing her to use her phone while she reads

53. Which of the following is the benefit of closure when planning a lesson?

a. To ensure the students are assessed properly
b. To ensure the students understand what was learned
c. To ensure the students can demonstrate their knowledge
d. To ensure the students understand forthcoming objectives

54. Which assistive technology is most appropriate for a student with a voice disorder that interferes with audible speech production?

a. Speech-to-text computer software
b. Text-to-speech computer software
c. Voice recognition computer software
d. Voice synthesizer computer software

55. Which of the following would be the greatest disadvantage of co-teaching?

a. One teacher may teach more than the other.
b. The teachers may disagree on strategies.
c. The teachers may not be experts in certain subjects.
d. One of the teachers may not have much experience.

56. Jack is a student who is being evaluated for special education services. He has been determined to have an orthopedic impairment and specific learning disability. Why might he not be eligible for the multiple disabilities category according to the Individuals with Disabilities Education Act (IDEA)?

a. Orthopedic impairment and specific learning disability have their own categories.
b. Autism spectrum disorders must be one of the disabilities in the multiple disability category.
c. The combination of these two disabilities does not increase needs beyond the individual disability categories.
d. Students with an orthopedic impairment are not eligible for the multiple disability category.

57. Mary is a 10-year-old student who has a developmental disability due to a physical impairment. Why would she NOT be eligible for special education services as a student with a developmental delay?

a. The developmental delay category does not include physical impairments.
b. The developmental delay category does not include students older than age 9.
c. The developmental delay category does not include students with developmental disabilities.
d. The developmental delay category does not include students younger than age 12.

58. A resource teacher can facilitate the greatest achievement in emergent writers who are scripting initial and final sounds by:

a. Suggesting they write a book to build confidence, teach sequencing, and encourage them to deeply explore ideas
b. Suggesting they read their stories to other students
c. Inviting a reporter to write about her emergent writers
d. Inviting parents or guardians for a tea party at which the children will read their stories aloud

59. Which of the following is a metacognitive learning strategy that aids in transferring learning to new, real-world situations?

a. Repetition
b. Learning to learn
c. Memorization
d. Passive listening

60. Which of the following best describes Down syndrome?

a. Gland malfunction
b. Dominant-gene transmission
c. Congenital deformity
d. Chromosomal difference

61. Jack is a fourth-grade student who is being assessed for another health impairment due to a diagnosis of attention deficit hyperactivity disorder, which affects his executive functioning abilities. Which assessment would MOST likely be included in this evaluation?

a. Behavior Rating Inventory of Executive Function
b. Cognitive Assessment System
c. Adaptive Behavior Inventory
d. Test of Problem-Solving

62. In facilitating reading comprehension and critical thinking in students with disabilities, which of the following strategies is best for visualizing concepts?

a. Teaching summarization
b. Using graphic organizers
c. Using multiple strategies
d. Teaching story structure

63. Which of the following is the best example of how a student with a specific learning disability can access standardized tests?

a. Allowing them to access alternate tests
b. Allowing them to access modified tests
c. Allowing them to access accommodated tests
d. Allowing them to access differentiated tests

64. Verbal dyspraxia is:

a. A motor skill development disorder that includes trouble with the physical act of writing
b. A motor skill development disorder that includes refusal to speak
c. A motor skill development disorder that includes misplacing letters within words
d. A motor skill development disorder that includes inconsistent speech errors

65. Tran is a student who recently arrived in the US from Vietnam. According to federal regulations mandated by the Individuals with Disabilities Education Act, which can be done if a learning disability is suspected?

a. Give Tran an IQ test to determine whether he has any specific learning disability.
b. Give Tran a reading evaluation test and a writing evaluation test, both in English.
c. Give Tran special education, depending on tests, with written parental consent.
d. Give Tran a written IEP for a learning disability regardless of the results of tests.

66. Brittany is a four-year-old preschool student who is administered a developmental assessment as part of her special education evaluation. Which of the following disability categories would LEAST likely be considered as a result of these assessments?

a. Development disability
b. Speech or language impairment
c. Specific learning disability
d. Autism spectrum disorder

67. Which of the following would determine a student to be ineligible for special education services as a student with a developmental delay?

a. A student with a delay in academic development
b. A student with a delay in social development
c. A student with a delay in adaptive development
d. A student with a delay in physical development

68. Which of the following is NOT true regarding students with visual perception LDs?

a. They have a higher rate of visual impairments than other students.
b. They are likely to miss words, sentences, or paragraphs in reading.
c. They can misinterpret facial expressions that transmit information.
d. They can have trouble differentiating among visually similar letters.

69. Jerry is an eighth grader with multiple disabilities. Why would it be beneficial for a teacher to construct a new test to assess Jerry rather than using standardized testing data?

a. Students with multiple disabilities do not take standardized tests.
b. Standardized data likely do not assess what Jerry has learned.
c. Accommodations are not allowed on standardized tests.
d. Jerry will not need standardized testing data for college admittance.

70. According to research findings, which of these is NOT a recommendation for improving the writing skills of students with learning disabilities?

a. Teaching students to set specific, attainable goals for writing
b. Teaching students strategies for planning, editing, and revising
c. Teaching students to avoid using writing for content learning
d. Teaching students how to use PC word processing programs

71. Which of the following is typically the most challenging when identifying whether an English learner qualifies for special education services?

a. It can be difficult to determine whether the student's difficulties are due to lack of mastery of the language or a disability.
b. The Individualized Education Program (IEP) may not meet their needs.
c. Special education services may not be beneficial in English.
d. The student may already miss too much class.

72. Which one of the following is NOT typically used to collect data as a curriculum-based assessment?

a. DIBELS
b. AIMSweb
c. EasyCBM
d. TerraNova

73. Which of the following strategies would be the LEAST productive when working with a disabled student whom you suspect to be a victim of abuse?

a. Listening to the student and trusting what they say
b. Reporting the suspicion to child services
c. Continuing to teach in the same manner to maintain status quo
d. Asking the child for more details on the incident

74. Which of the following pieces of adaptive equipment could help ALL of the following students: one with hearing impairment, one with communication deficits, one with cognitive deficits, and one with fine-motor skills deficits?

a. A computer with a touch screen
b. A classroom amplification system
c. A large-print book/books on tape
d. A word processor with voice output

75. Which of the following checks for understanding would be most appropriate when teaching a small-group writing lesson to seventh graders?

a. Using whiteboards
b. Using self-assessments
c. Using cooperative learning
d. Using flip charts

76. A resource room teacher has a small group of second and third graders who are struggling with reading comprehension. The most effective strategy would be to:

a. Present a list of vocabulary words before students read a particular text.
b. Ask students to create a play about the story.
c. Read a story aloud. Ask students to raise their hands when they hear an unfamiliar word.
d. Have each child keep a book of new vocabulary words. Whenever an unfamiliar word is seen or heard, the student should enter the word in this personal dictionary.

77. Which one of the following education service providers gives instructional assistance to students who receive special education services?

a. Teaching assistants
b. Paraprofessionals
c. Student teachers
d. Behavior support professionals

78. Jadon is a second-grade student with a goal in written expression. Which of the following curriculum-based assessments would be most appropriate in assessing his progress on his written expression goal?

a. Giving him 10 minutes to write an essay
b. Giving him 3 minutes to write spelling words
c. Giving him 3 minutes to write a paragraph
d. Giving him 1 minute to write a sentence

79. Which of the following is true regarding teaching spelling?

a. Students who have an understanding of letter-sound association do not need to be taught to spell. If they can sound out a word, they can spell it.
b. Students who are able to determine the origin of a root word (Latin, Greek, Indo-European, etc.) can usually deduce the correct spelling of a word and do not require direct instruction in spelling.
c. Drilling spelling exercises is the most effective long-term method of teaching spelling.
d. By applying spelling patterns found in word families, the spelling of many words can be deduced.

80. Brady is a second-grade student working on reading fluency. Which of the following would be the best example for a demonstration of learning at the end of the lesson?

a. Asking Brady to read a story and answer questions
b. Asking Brady to listen to a short reading passage
c. Asking Brady to read a timed short reading passage
d. Asking Brady to read a list of words with assistance

Answer Key and Explanations for Test #1

1. C: Before evaluating him for special education services, it is best to see if his struggles are related to his lack of English skills or if he might have a disability. Testing him right away makes it difficult to make that determination without putting some interventions in place. It is best practice to wait and see what steps need to be taken first. Answer A is incorrect because English learners are eligible for special education services if they are determined to be eligible. Answer B is incorrect because he may or may not have a disability at all. Answer D is incorrect because although it may take him a while to learn the curriculum, this is not necessary in order to evaluate a student for special education.

2. A: Although standardized tests can have many functions and be used in a variety of ways, they are designed to compare a student's score with what the average student scores. These can be beneficial in determining whether or not a student is keeping up with their peers in academic areas. Students with disabilities will often take the same standardized tests as their peers, but it is important to understand the areas that they struggle in and how to help them. Answer B is incorrect because progress is typically monitored through measures such as curriculum-based assessments. Answer C is incorrect because finding strengths and weaknesses in a student's development is an example of a developmental assessment. Answer D is incorrect because intellectual ability is typically measured using an IQ test.

3. C: Although it is not always easy or possible to eliminate every bias that a person might have, it is important not to make any assumptions. It is important to be sensitive to student needs especially when working with students with disabilities or from various cultural backgrounds. Assessments should be geared toward the content that students should know rather than the opinions that a teacher may have. Answer A is incorrect because it may not always be possible or realistic to get to know the background of every student in the class. Answer B is incorrect because each assessment will be different, and it may not be possible or the best assessment of student knowledge to include multicultural questions. Answer D is incorrect because it is not appropriate or the best practice to evaluate each student differently.

4. C: Although all of these choices relate to science and can be functional for certain students, learning how to maintain a garden is the best example of a functional curriculum. A functional curriculum is designed to provide opportunities for students to work on their independent living skills. Maintaining a garden is a valuable skill that can be helpful for students like Brian to learn and apply once they graduate high school. The other answer choices are primarily academic and less tied to independent living or vocational skills.

5. C: Although all these choices may be beneficial to students who struggle with organizational skills, data managers are the most effective in helping students organize tasks. These data managers allow students to put information on tasks into a system, and the system is instrumental in organizing it for them. Students with executive functioning skills can benefit from these tools in that they have to do less of the organization and management of information. Answer A is incorrect because FM listening devices are typically for students who struggle with hearing. Answer B is incorrect because speech recognition programs are designed for students who struggle with writing texts. Answer D is incorrect because abbreviation expanders are beneficial in helping students who may struggle with word processing.

6. A: Students are eligible to receive support for each one of the disability categories that they are identified in. Because of this, Trevor can receive academic support as a student with a specific learning disability and emotional support as a student with an emotional disturbance. Although students do not necessarily need to be identified as having more than one eligibility category to receive these supports, the identification of each one of these allows the IEP team to formally address both needs when determining mandatory services. Answer B is incorrect because Trevor would not automatically be eligible for a self-contained classroom. Answer C is incorrect because Trevor can have a behavior plan without being identified with co-occurring conditions. Answer D is incorrect because alternative placement is not determined based on co-occurring conditions.

7. C: In planning lessons, teachers need to consider the skill or concept they want to teach and be sure to define it and not assume they already know what it is (A). They need to identify the prerequisites that students need to learn the new material, not assume that they already have them (B). They need to consider what is required for the students to master the material being taught (C). They should also think about how they can expand what they have taught and how to show students to apply their new learning in useful ways. Such planning is not premature (D) and should be part of the lesson plans.

8. D: All students determined eligible for Special Education services must have an IEP. In writing it, educators must include the student's present level of functioning. To decide what the student needs to learn, by when, and how it will be measured, educators must establish baseline scores. Retesting with the same instruments after a period of intervention and comparing scores will show if the intervention is effective if scores improve. To make developmentally appropriate placement decisions, educators must know at what levels the student currently performs. While the results of an evaluation can be used to determine eligibility for Special Education Services, they are not used to make medical diagnoses.

9. D: Books in large print and on teen-related topics but with simplified text are the ideal combination for Clyde's visual impairment, age, and reading comprehension level. Therefore, option D is correct.

Large-print books are a good idea for Clyde's visual impairment, and subjects relevant to teens are appropriate for his age, but not for his first-grade reading level. Therefore, option A is incorrect.

Children's books have the large print and simple subject matter Clyde needs, but they are not appropriate for his age. Therefore, option B is incorrect.

With the availability of large-print textbooks, a magnifying glass is not the easiest way for Clyde to read. Having one would certainly expand the types of media he could see, and it would be beneficial for him to have it if he should want or need to see the small print in everyday media like newspapers and phone books. But for reading, it would not be as easy on his eyes as large print. Also, many books with regular-size print will be beyond Clyde's first-grade level of reading comprehension. Therefore, option C is incorrect.

10. D: It is likely not going to be useful to change curriculum for the next unit because of the performance of students. It will be more beneficial to take a look at some of the instructional strategies used and if there were ways to make the learning more meaningful and productive for the students being tested. This is especially the case for students with disabilities and meeting the needs of each student in the class. Answer A is incorrect because determining which kinds of questions that students struggled with can allow the teacher to redesign or modify those questions for the next test. Answer B is incorrect because identifying which students struggled allows the teacher to keep a closer eye on or accommodate some of these students. Answer C is incorrect because understanding the kinds of questions that the students asked can help to fill some of the holes that might have been left throughout the teaching.

11. C: Although these are examples of assistive technology devices, the FM listening system is typically used for students to listen to the speech of someone else. Students like George who struggle with writing will likely benefit more from devices that can help with the writing process. Assistive technology can be beneficial in helping students to access the general education curriculum despite their disability. Answer A is incorrect because graphic organizers can be helpful for students who struggle to start the writing process. Answer B is incorrect because proofreading programs can review what students have written. Answer D is incorrect because word-prediction programs can help predict what a student may want to write.

12. C: Formative assessments are used to monitor the students during instruction to provide feedback. This way, the teacher can make changes to the lesson plans as necessary or fill holes in the gaps of student knowledge. Answer A is incorrect because a test at the end of the unit would be considered a summative assessment. Answer B is incorrect because a test before the unit would be considered a diagnostic assessment. Answer D is incorrect because monitoring his behavior during tests would be completed after the unit rather than throughout it.

13. D: Carefully planning what the content of the math instruction covers and the order in which it is taught (A), using their best judgment in choosing and applying appropriate teaching strategies (B), and designing practice activities with a wide range of student needs in mind (C) are all actions by teachers that will improve the involvement and progress of all students, including those with special needs. The action most likely to be needed specifically by some special needs students in the general education classroom is using more intensive direct instruction methods to teach them basic mathematics.

14. C: It is recommended that teachers should offer alternative explanations for math facts instead of rote learning. For example, instead of simply having students keep trying to memorize the times tables, a teacher can explain that if 3 x 2 = 6, and 4 is twice as much as 2, then 3 x 4 is twice as much as 3 x 2, so 3 x 4 = 12 because twice as much as 6 = 12. Students should not be discouraged from using estimates; experts recommend that teachers encourage students with dyscalculia to practice their estimating skills as a way to initiate the solution of math problems. It is not recommended for teachers to move from abstract to concrete examples when presenting new material; educators advise they begin with concrete examples, which are more accessible, and progress as warranted to more abstract problems. Recommendations do not state that students should not have to use graph paper if organizing things on paper is hard for them; experts actually advise giving them graph paper to facilitate this process.

15. D: Students with executive functioning deficits often struggle to organize their thoughts or stay focused . Providing them with daily objectives allows them the opportunity to understand what is expected of them and to remain on task. It is important to continually review the objectives throughout the lesson so that students are reminded of what is expected. Answer A is incorrect because planning can be a difficult skill for students with executive functioning deficits. Answer B is incorrect because objectives typically are not designed as an assessment method. Answer C is incorrect because an objective is a goal that the task should help the student achieve—not an extra task.

16. D: The student could most benefit from focusing on comprehension, as this would most directly improve her difficulties with understanding what she reads. Fluency pertains to the ability to speak or write a language, which is not an issue mentioned in the question. Since the student reads words accurately, she likely does not need to focus on vocabulary. Phonics teaches the relationship between sounds and written symbols. This would not target the student's problems with understanding.

17. C: According to research (e.g., Heller, UI Chicago, 2010), the generation that has received school services mandated by the IDEA has accordingly come to expect more support throughout life, including support for being able to grow older at home. This support is more necessary because life expectancies for the developmentally disabled (DD) have increased similarly to those for others (A). Although the majority of DD adults live with their families, only roughly 5% of funding for DD is used for family support (B). Research finds adults with DDs are more likely to develop chronic health problems (D).

18. C: Before being referred for special education services, the team must provide intensive interventions to see how Freddy responds to those. Answer A is incorrect because the team must provide more support before evaluating for special education. Answer B is incorrect because continuing to provide the remediation likely will not work, as there have been no improvements. Answer D is incorrect because removing the remediation would likely cause Freddy to struggle more.

19. B: When writing learning objectives, it is important that they are specific to the needs of the student, measurable or quantifiable, appropriately attainable for the group of students, relevant to the current topic or lesson, and include a timeframe for the student to achieve the goal. Answers A, C, and D are incorrect because they are each missing some of these SMART components.

20. B: The COACH model (Giangreco, Cloninger, and Iverson 1998) is a collaborative approach described by educational researchers as "student-directed planning," which they claim goes "beyond person-centered planning" (Wehmeyer et al. 2002) by making the student central in the process. Person-centered planning typically centers more on family and social support systems. GAP (Turnbull & Turnbull 2002) (A); MAPs (Pearpoint, Forest, and O'Brien 1996) (C); and PATH (D), which extends the MAPs process to develop "a more definitive plan of action," are all examples of person-centered planning.

21. D: In order to measure reading fluency, it is essential to provide a student with a reading passage and record how many words they can read in one minute. This can help to determine how much progress a student has made and what they may still need to work on. Reading fluency is an important skill for a third grader to practice each day by reading passages and developing a clear understanding of words. Answer A is incorrect because identifying letters is a skill that students typically work on before third grade. Answer B is incorrect because although identifying letter sounds can be important, it is not always the best indicator of reading fluency ability. Answer C is incorrect because although reading sight words can help with reading fluency skills, it is not a measure of reading fluency by itself.

22. C: Typically, the special education teacher will collaborate with school counselors and administrators about what the best placement for students may be, but they aren't solely responsible for coming up with the class schedule. Answer A is incorrect because managing paraprofessionals is an important task for the special education teacher. Answer B is incorrect because scheduling IEP meetings with the parent is also an important task. Answer D is incorrect because it is important for the special education teacher to help support the general education teacher in regard to ways to help students with IEPs.

23. C: If a student like Pat has been receiving services enough to collect a sufficient amount of data, a special education referral is warranted. If Pat has not made much progress in his reading fluency for six weeks, it is possible that he has a disability. It is important to give the student enough time to access the interventions and see if any kind of progress is made before referring the student to special education. Answer A is incorrect because although the length of the intervention may vary for certain students, six weeks is typically sufficient. Answer B is incorrect because discontinuing interventions may be detrimental to Pat as he continues to struggle with reading fluency. Answer D is incorrect because referral to a 504 plan would likely not be warranted because special education may be more appropriate given Pat's needs.

24. D: Out of the options given, modifying the content can help the most with her reading comprehension struggles. Modifying the content to include less reading or fewer questions she has to answer still allows her to learn most, if not all, of what her peers learn. It is important to understand how to provide support in a way that students can still learn what their general education peers are learning whenever possible. Answer A is incorrect because it may alienate Anna to move her down a grade level. Answer B is incorrect because although reteaching concepts may be beneficial, her time with the special education teacher may be better spent working on her reading comprehension abilities. Answer C is incorrect because providing support from a paraprofessional likely would not be as beneficial as modifying the curriculum.

25. D: Although all these methods may be helpful in measuring a student's behavior needs, using random time samples can be beneficial in determining the frequency of the behavior. Random time samples allow teachers to observe the student at various times throughout the day to determine the cause and frequency of these behaviors. This can be measured to determine how much progress the student is making on their goals. Answer A is incorrect because curriculum-based measures tend to be more effective for students with academic goals. Answer B is incorrect because it may be difficult to measure how a student compares to their peers. Answer C is incorrect because simply counting the number of referrals likely does not provide sufficient data.

26. D: Although it is possible that all of these choices can be beneficial in certain circumstances, an 11th-grade student tutoring a 9th grader is the most appropriate. It is important for the students to be close in age to be considered peers and for the tutor to be mature. For students with disabilities who are being tutored, it is also best if the student who is tutoring is the same age or older to avoid having a student who is lacking confidence. Answer A is incorrect because a student in 2nd grade may or may not be mature enough to tutor another student. Answer B is incorrect because the peer tutor model tends to work better when the students are closer in age. Answer C is incorrect because it is best to have the tutor be someone who is older or the same age as the student who needs the tutoring.

27. A: Adaptive behavior scales are designed to assess how well students do with daily and basic living skills. Cognition is not something that would be assessed by one of these kinds of assessments. Answer B is incorrect because communicating with others is an important skill for students to possess after school ends. Answer C is incorrect because motor skills must be evaluated to determine what support a student may need. Answer D is incorrect because social skills are important to have in the community when working with others.

28. C: The best alternative would be the inner hallway outside the behavior specialists' office. Being an inner hallway, it is likely to be quieter. During class hours, most professionals' offices in this hall are empty as their occupants are doing training or monitoring in classrooms, making rounds, etc. In contrast, the hallway outside the classroom is likely to be noisy during class times, with more traffic and less privacy. Lee's living area upstairs is farther away, requiring more transport time, and the behavior specialists would also have to bring all the testing materials. Inside the classroom, even off in a corner, is not a good location as the class activities can distract Lee from testing, and testing can disrupt the classroom activities and distract the students and teacher as well as violate the student's privacy and confidentiality.

29. D: Educational testing tools (D) are used to determine a student's current achievement in academic subjects. Cognitive test instruments (A) are given as part of the psychological evaluation and determine cognitive development and abilities rather than academic achievement. A sociocultural evaluation (B) is usually made by a school social worker, often by interviewing parents, to establish a developmental history and collect information about environmental influences. Behavioral observations (C) are used to gather data about a student's behaviors, often to aid in making a functional behavior analysis that may inform a behavior intervention plan, but would not determine academic achievement levels.

30. B: Meeting Edgar directly allows you to form your own impressions based on who he is, rather than relying on paperwork or others' perspectives, which helps reduce bias. Getting to know more about him and his background will provide more information so you have a better idea of how to meet his needs. Answer A is incorrect because simply reading his IEP will not give you as much personal information about who he is as a person. Answer C is incorrect because calling his parents might be helpful, but it is important to have a relationship with the student. Answer D is incorrect because knowing his history also will not help you with personal information.

31. B: Regional and magnet schools for deaf students currently only exist in a few locations in the country, so students often have to live away from home to attend them. This would not be an example of inclusive education. Therefore, option B is correct.

Attending general education schools and being pulled out for special education instruction is one inclusive solution for deaf students. Therefore, option A is incorrect.

Teaching sign language to all students and teachers in the general education setting is another inclusive strategy. Therefore, option C is incorrect.

Assigning interpreters to the classrooms for deaf students who use sign language is another inclusive strategy. Therefore, option D is incorrect.

32. A: Developmental assessments are designed to find strengths and weaknesses in young students who may be exhibiting some delays. In order to do this, students are compared with what the average student is capable of doing in many developmental categories. These assessments can be effective in intervening in students early who may be struggling. Answer B is incorrect because a quick identifying assessment that would be used is typically referred to as a screener. Answer C is incorrect because a behavior rating scale typically identifies just the behavior of students of all ages. Answer D is incorrect because an alternative assessment is typically used for students with disabilities who cannot access standardized tests.

33. B: Modern society demands greater literacy today than in the past. For example, as cited by Dr. Rebecca C. Faulkner, the Air Force manual for repairing fighter planes was seven pages long in World War II and 7,000 pages long in 2008. The same literacy skills in students do not apply across all subjects (A) because different literacy skills are needed for different content areas. Literacy required of school pupils also does not stay constant across grades (C) because literacy requirements advance along with each advance in grade level. Finally, literacy is not best taught in schools as a separate lesson (D) because that would be insufficient; in order to meet the changing demands of society, literacy must be taught and incorporated throughout the school day.

34. D: Although all these choices can have positive and negative impacts, high school students commonly have the strongest social influences on academic engagement and performance coming from their peer groups. As a student enters high school, the locus of influence frequently moves from family involvement to friends. That said, when a child comes from a household in which both parents are present and supportive, it can have a huge impact on the access they have to educational support. Children who have little support in the home or come from broken homes have a high chance of struggling academically. The locus of influence for students is extremely variable, however, so it is important that teachers recognize that not all students will have a strong influence from either peer groups or family, and each student should be considered individually.

35. A: Generalization of learning is the ability to apply learning across multiple and varied contexts or settings. Regular practice and periodic testing (B) are designed to promote maintenance rather than generalization. Learning one step at a time (C) is a characteristic of task analysis, which breaks complex skills or tasks down into more achievable steps and is related to promoting skill acquisition rather than generalization. Practicing a new skill before applying it to real-life situations (D) is a way to promote both acquisition and maintenance of the skill before its application and generalization.

36. B: A Renaissance festival would be crowded and noisy, with many different smells, sights, and sounds. The magnitude and variety of sensory stimuli would be overwhelming to most individuals with autism. Therefore, option A is incorrect.

A nature hike is likely to be in a quiet and tranquil environment. With plants as the main sensory stimuli, an autistic individual would have the opportunity to focus on examining them closely. Many autistic individuals are susceptible to sensory overload from environmental stimuli; many are also very good at focused, circumscribed activities wherein they can apply their intellectual abilities to specific tasks. Therefore, option B is correct.

A community mixer is a social event. Most people with autism have difficulty with social interactions. Typically, they have difficulty recognizing and interpreting social cues such as facial expressions and body language. In addition to the social emphasis, a mixer would also be noisy and crowded, which would be over-stimulating to an autistic student. Therefore, option C is incorrect.

A rock concert would involve over-amplified music, which can be painful to many individuals with autism. And it would be crowded with many people. Therefore, option D is incorrect.

37. A: Although all of these choices may be effective in certain situations, tally marks would likely be most beneficial in recording the number of outbursts. Tally marks can assist the teacher in determining the number of outbursts that the student has over a period of time. These tally marks can be used to identify when or where these outbursts are occurring and how they can be prevented. Answer B is incorrect because although time sampling can be helpful for certain student behaviors, outbursts are best measured using tally marks. Answers C and D involve qualitative data that are very useful for understanding the context and triggers of Matthew's outbursts, but they are time-consuming and harder to summarize numerically for frequent formative progress monitoring. Tally marks (frequency recording) give the teacher simple, countable data to track whether the number of outbursts is increasing or decreasing over time.

38. D: Extended school year services are provided to students who struggle to retain information over the course of long breaks such as the summer. Some students who are determined eligible for these services receive addition schooling, typically sometime in the summer. This allows the students to retain some of the skills that they may forget over the course of extended breaks. Answer A is incorrect because not all students are determined eligible for extended school year services. Answer B is incorrect because there is not a set time period in which the services must be provided. Answer C is incorrect because extended school year services are typically provided sometime in the summer and not necessarily before the school year starts.

39. C: Students who receive services in the multiple disabilities category cannot be eligible in just one disability category. These students have more than one disability that impacts them to the point that one category does not meet their needs. According to IDEA, the combination of disabilities makes it so severe that they cannot be accommodated in one category. Answer A is incorrect because deaf-blindness has its own disability category. Answer B is incorrect because a student with an orthopedic impairment can be eligible for the multiple disabilities category if they are impacted by another disability as well. Answer D is incorrect because the impact of disabilities may change, and students can go from being identified as a student with multiple disabilities to a single disability over time.

40. D: Enthusiastically accepted. The adults discuss a background check and the possibility the teen might discover gardening is not for her and want to quit. However, this is most likely to occur early in her employment, giving the neighbor sufficient time to find another helper. The teacher is pleased because the girl will learn new skills through modeling and repetition. The mother is pleased because the experience will add to the girl's self-esteem and show her she is capable of learning. The elderly neighbor is pleased because she is both compassionate and truly needs help. The girl is delighted the neighbor recognizes her potential and sees her as valuable.

41. C: Although some of these choices may be true in certain situations, parents of students with disabilities will typically see some of the signs before the child is evaluated at school. The parents likely spend a good deal of time with these children, so they are aware of what they can and can't do. They may not know for certain whether or not a student has a disability, but they can determine what they struggle with at home. Answer A is incorrect because families of children with disabilities are more likely to experience issues than they are to come together. Answer B is incorrect because parents are not the cause of the learning disability and also cannot be the cure. Answer D is incorrect because while some families do often seek out information to learn more about disabilities, this is not as consistently seen as families suspecting a disability is present in a child before the school does.

42. A: One of the health problems that is included in the other health impairment category, according to the Individuals with Disabilities Education Act (IDEA), is asthma. A student with an other health impairment has limited strength, vitality, or alertness due to an acute or chronic health problem. If a student has an acute or chronic case of asthma that impacts his or her ability to function in the educational environment, the student may be eligible for the other health impairment category. Answer B is incorrect because cerebral palsy would fall into the "orthopedic impairment" category. Answer C is incorrect because traumatic brain injury has its own category. Answer D is incorrect because a student with a perceptual disability would fall under the "specific learning disability" category.

43. C: Although all of these choices can be valuable in enhancing the learning experience for students in the class, creating experiences that they will enjoy and remember will likely have the greatest impact on the majority of students. A meaningful learning experience will likely include topics that the students enjoy and topics that they will remember. Students with disabilities will especially be more likely to take meaning from topics that they are interested in. Answer A is incorrect because although offering to help can certainly benefit the students, they may or may not find this meaningful to them. Answer B is incorrect because although getting to know each student can help them feel safe and secure in the class, this may not impact the meaning of the class. Answer D is incorrect because giving rewards to students may not have as much of a long-term impact on the students.

44. D: These are all examples of AT (d) that could be used in assessment. Not all AT need be "high-tech." A pencil wrapped with tape (a) could assist a student who has difficulty grasping writing implements in completing a written questionnaire. A text-to-speech-enabled computer (b) could assist students whose speech is impaired or absent, who have difficulty with verbal interactions, or have visual impairments, in responding to test questions or items. A computer's word processing program (c) can assist students with dysgraphia (writing disability), as well as problems with spelling, vocabulary, syntax, processing, and so on in responding to test items.

45. B: IDEA requires at least one general education teacher to be on a student's IEP team. The other answer choices list individuals who may be members of an IEP team in certain situations, but they are not required by law to be on the team.

46. A: Well-organized coaching in decoding, sight words, vocabulary and comprehension several times a week would be the most beneficial to improve this student's reading comprehension. The more systematic the lessons are, the better the chance the intervention will succeed.

47. B: Spending half the period with one student is not an efficient use of time. The extra attention does not speed up Jonathan's response time so it does not benefit him and it deprives other students of Ms. Lewis' attention. Therefore option A is incorrect.

Ms. Lewis should give the benefit of her instructional skills equally to all students. It is a good use of the aide's time to monitor Jonathan. She can make sure he is on task and let Ms. Lewis know when he has made a response. She can then monitor and help whichever other students Ms. Lewis is not working with at the time. Therefore option B is correct.

The fact that Corey and Jennifer simply work at the same speed is not a valid reason for Ms. Lewis to spend all her time with them, although it might be convenient. Each student should get equal time. Therefore option C is incorrect.

Though Michelle needs individual attention to stay focused, this does not mean Ms. Lewis should spend all her time with her. The aide can monitor and help her when Ms. Lewis is working with other students. Therefore option D is incorrect.

48. B: According to US federal law, Teddy cannot be judged as disabled solely because he is illiterate. IDEA stipulates that a student "....must not be determined to be a child with a disability under 34 CFR Part 300 if the determinant factor...is lack of appropriate instruction in reading...as defined in...the ESEA [or]...in math...." The ESEA is the Elementary and Secondary Education Act of 1965. Title I of this act was amended in 2001 by the No Child Left Behind Act, which is also referred to in IDEA documents as the ESEA. Teddy may not be determined to be functionally disabled. It is not true that he cannot receive remedial education for his illiteracy. It is only true that he cannot be classified as having a disability because of it. He can still receive remedial teaching that will eventually bring his skills up to the appropriate age/grade level.

49. D: The XBA approach can enhance comprehensiveness by allowing use of subtests from different test instruments focusing on the same cognitive and/or academic area(s). It also enhances selectivity and depth by allowing selection from different batteries of subtests most relevant to the student's presenting difficulties. Researchers have found this approach useful for assessing reading and writing disorders, but this is not its sole or primary use; and this approach is evidence-based (A), as research evidence supports its application. The XBA approach assesses across domains of both academic (B) and intellectual (C) performance.

50. B: Although all these choices can be helpful strategies for students who are at risk, providing a caring and supportive classroom environment is most likely to be effective. Many of these students do not have much positive support in their lives and need someone that they can trust and rely on. Although it may be difficult for these students to open up and talk, it is important that they have a caring classroom setting and someone that they can turn to when they need to talk. Answer A is incorrect because simply giving them accommodations may not provide them with enough support to be successful. Answer C is incorrect because requiring peer collaboration without a supportive climate may not be effective for students who are hesitant to engage. Answer D is incorrect because providing opportunities for after-school activities does not directly influence the classroom climate.

51. B: Playing "I Spy" looking for each letter in the alphabet (B) is not a way to teach phonological awareness, although it is a way to teach children alphabet knowledge. The jump-rope game "A my name is Alice" (A) is a way to teach phonological awareness by demonstrating similarities in initial word sounds within sentence patterns and using rhythm. Singing Shirley Ellis's song "The Name Game" (C) teaches phonological awareness by demonstrating similarities and differences in initial word sounds, discrimination among sounds, practicing rhymes, using repetition, and making it fun with the use of nonsense syllables and music. Reading Dr. Seuss books to and with children (D) teaches phonological awareness, as the author made extensive use of rhyming and repetition, reinforcing these with humor, imaginary creatures and names, and wonderful illustrations.

52. B: For a student with reading comprehension difficulties, audiobooks can reduce the cognitive load of decoding so she can focus on understanding the story, especially when paired with explicit comprehension strategies. Answer A is incorrect because simply researching her topic may not help her with reading. Answer C is incorrect because although giving a presentation may be beneficial, it is still important for her to read the content. Answer D is incorrect because allowing her to use her phone may be too distracting.

53. B: It is important to have closure in a lesson so students have a firm grasp on the concepts they were expected to learn that particular day. Closure gives the students clarity if there was any confusion about what they were supposed to learn. Students with disabilities may need extra reminders, and closure can help with this. Answer a is incorrect because closure typically happens before or after the assessment as a method of recapping what was taught. Answer c is incorrect because the demonstration of knowledge is typically a task that the student completes so the teacher knows that they understood the task. Answer d is incorrect because although closure may connect to objectives that may be coming in the future, it mostly relates to the tasks completed within that day.

54. D: Computer software with a voice synthesizer produces a digital voice for those who cannot speak. Most of the time, a student who needs this type of assistance will have a device called an augmentative and alternative communication (AAC) device that contains the software and hardware needed to run a voice synthesizer for real-time communications. This differs from text-to-speech software in that AACs contain special programming that allow the user to quickly string together words for real-time communication. Text-to-speech software requires typing and is not accessible enough to function in real communication for most people. Speech-to-text software (A) allows a person to speak into a computer microphone and the program produces typed text of the spoken language. This helps those who can speak but cannot write or type. Text-to-speech software (B) also produces a synthesized voice to read text, but these programs typically scan the text and read it aloud to assist those with visual impairments and reading difficulties, not to supply a substitute speaking voice. Voice recognition software (C) also transcribes spoken language into typed text, similar to the closed-captioning feature on televisions.

55. B: Although all of these choices could be potential conflicts in the co-teaching model, disagreeing on strategies is likely the greatest disadvantage. When teachers collaborate to teach a class, the general education teacher and special education teacher may have different approaches to certain topics and tasks. This may lead to some conflicts about the instructional strategies or how some of the students learn best. Answer A is incorrect because typically co-teaching will involve one teacher teaching more than the other. Answer C is incorrect because it is best to collaborate in subjects that teachers are familiar with in order to provide students with the best possible instruction. Answer D is incorrect because even if one teacher does not have as much experience, it is still possible to collaborate and learn from one another.

56. C: According to the IDEA, the multiple disabilities category is for students who are affected by multiple disabilities in which the combination of those disabilities severely affects their educational needs beyond what can be accommodated by one of the qualifying categories. Answer A is incorrect; although they do have their own category, they can still be considered for multiple disabilities. Answer B is incorrect because autism is not required for the multiple disabilities category. Answer D is incorrect because students with an orthopedic impairment can be eligible for multiple disabilities.

57. B: In order to be eligible for the developmental delay category, students must be age 9 or younger. There are many impairments that are included within the category, but students must be a certain age. According to IDEA, a student like Mary would likely be eligible in a different category because of her developmental disability. Answer A is incorrect because the developmental delay category does include students with physical impairments. Answer C is incorrect because students with developmental disabilities such as physical or emotional impairments would be eligible for the category if they meet the age requirements. Answer D is incorrect because students younger than age 10 are included in the category.

58. B: A resource teacher can accomplish this by suggesting they read their stories to other students. Emergent writers scripting initial and final sounds will gain the most immediate and relevant satisfaction by moving around the room, reading what they've written to other students.

59. B: Learning to learn is one of the most valuable skills or learning strategies for the real-world environment. It helps students understand how they learn, check their own progress, and adjust their strategies. When teachers lecture, students are often taught facts but are not taught how to incorporate the facts into real life situations. Using the strategy of learning to learn teaches students how to solve problems and think critically. Additionally, when this method is combined with group learning, students learn how to interact with others in a team environment, which enhances leadership skills. While repetition and memorization are useful strategies for learning, learning to learn aids in implementing the strategies that work for the student and the student's specific situation.

60. D: Down syndrome, which is caused by the presence of an extra chromosome, is the most frequent cause of intellectual disabilities in infancy.

61. A: The Behavior Rating Inventory of Executive Function test is used to identify behaviors that affect a student's performance in the classroom and includes executive functioning. Answer B is incorrect because the Cognitive Assessment System is a test that measures a student's cognitive processing abilities. Answer C is incorrect because the Adaptive Behavior Inventory is used to identify which independent living skills a student may struggle with. Answer D is incorrect because the Test of Problem-Solving is used to assess students with communication needs.

62. B: Graphic organizers depict ideas and information in a variety of ways, and all of them are visual (e.g., charts, maps, pictures, etc.). These can be very helpful to students with disabilities who have trouble comprehending abstract concepts or organizing information because they make the material more concrete by using another modality. Teaching students how to summarize (A) helps them identify the important points or themes in reading material, and teaching them how to analyze the structure of a story (D) aids reading comprehension while employing critical thinking. Both of these skills will not directly make information visual unless they are taught specifically using graphic organizers (which include semantic organizers/maps). Using multiple strategies (C) is always highly recommended, but such strategies may involve a range of modalities, not simply a visual one.

63. C: For students with specific learning disabilities, it is important that they are able to access standardized tests to determine what kind of progress they are making. In order for them to access these tests, oftentimes they will need to be provided accommodations. These accommodations allow them to access the same test as their general education peers. Answer A is incorrect because alternative tests are typically for students who cannot access the standardized test even with accommodations. Answer B is incorrect because standardized tests do not typically allow modifications to the tests. Answer D is incorrect because differentiation would be an example of something that would be done in a classroom setting rather than on a standardized test.

64. D: Verbal dyspraxia is a motor skill development disorder which includes speech errors that don't clearly follow a pattern and so appear to be inconsistent. An example is a student who can pronounce /p/ when it is followed by a long i, as in pine, but not when followed by an ou diphthong, as in pout. Verbally dyspraxic individuals are unable to correctly place the tongue, lips and jaw for consistent sounds that can be organized into syllables. Dyspraxia appears to be a brain disorder in which the area that controls production of particular sounds is damaged.

65. C: Following evaluation, if a learning disability is identified, the school can only give Tran special education services with the written permission of his parents. Therefore, option C is correct.

An IQ test alone cannot be given because no single test can be used to identify a disability. All areas of any suspected disability must be evaluated. Therefore, option A is incorrect.

The Individuals with Disabilities Education Act (IDEA) 2004 stipulates that tests must be given in the child's native language, must measure a disability rather than limited English language skills, and must not discriminate on a racial or cultural basis. A reading test and writing test, both in English, would violate these rules. Therefore, option B is incorrect.

The school cannot write an IEP for Tran regardless of his test results. IDEA specifies that, to benefit from the educational program, Tran must be found to have a specific learning disability as well as a need for special education services. Following Tran's evaluation, a multidisciplinary team meeting should be held to develop an IEP. This meeting would include Tran's parents. Therefore, option D is incorrect.

66. C: Developmental assessments typically do not include tests that would determine a student eligible for a specific learning disability. Although these developmental assessments are beneficial in determining what a student may struggle with, it is difficult to determine the academic skills of children at such a young age. Specific learning disabilities typically manifest as students have had more instruction in reading, writing, and math. Answer A is incorrect because the developmental disability category is common for preschool students who are struggling in certain developmental areas. Answer B is incorrect because speech or language impairments are also common with preschool students. Answer D is incorrect because students with a diagnosis of autism are often identified in the autism spectrum disorder category as a preschooler.

67. A: A student with an academic delay would not be eligible for the "developmental delay" category, according to IDEA. The category includes many areas, but it does not specify academics as one of them. The criteria include cognitive development but do not use the term "academic development." Answer B is incorrect because a student with a social development delay would be eligible according to IDEA criteria. Answer C is incorrect because adaptive delays are also listed under the IDEA definition. Answer D is incorrect because a delay in physical development would also determine a child to be eligible as a student with a developmental delay.

68. A: It is not true that students with visual perception LDs (A) have a higher rate of visual impairments than other students. Difficulties with visual perception occur in the brain areas that interpret visual signals, not with the sensory ability of eyesight. Students with visual perception problems can have perfect vision. This LD makes students likely to miss words, sentences, or entire paragraphs when they are reading (B). Students with this type of LD can also misunderstand others' facial expressions that communicate such things (C) as disbelief, approval, boredom, or indicating that a conversation is over. Another common effect of a visual perception LD is having difficulty telling apart similar-looking letters (D), numbers, characters, or symbols. Perceiving letters backwards or distorted also frequently occurs with this type of LD.

69. B: Although standardized testing data can be valuable for certain students, many students with disabilities are learning an alternate curriculum. Alternative testing is available for some students, but teachers may find that constructing a new test is more beneficial in assessing what a student is capable of. This can be helpful in determining how much progress a student has made over the year or what the student still needs help with. Answer A is incorrect because students with multiple disabilities can still take the standardized tests with accommodations or alternative assessments. Answer C is incorrect because accommodations are typically allowed on standardized tests for students with disabilities. Answer D is incorrect because although Jerry may or may not attend college, standardized data can still be helpful.

70. C: Research has found that using writing as a tool for learning academic content is helpful to normally achieving students and students with learning disabilities (LD), so teaching students to avoid this (C) is not a recommendation. Based on their findings, researchers recommend teaching students to set specific, attainable goals for what they will write (A). They advise teachers to instruct students in strategies for planning what they will write, editing what they have written, and making indicated revisions (B). Researchers also recommend that teachers give LD students instruction in using PC word processing programs (D), which can make many aspects of writing much easier for them.

71. A: One of the challenges of identifying students who receive English learner services for special education is deciding whether or not their needs are related to a disability. It can be difficult to distinguish between a student with a disability and a student who is new to the language. It is crucial to take all of the steps that are necessary to ensure the correct placement of these students. Answer B is incorrect because if it is determined that a student is eligible for special education services, the IEP must meet their needs. Answer C is incorrect because special education services would be beneficial in providing the student access to the general education curriculum. Answer D is incorrect because the decision is based on whether or not services are needed for special education rather than the services they already received.

72. D: TerraNova is an example of a standardized test rather than a curriculum-based assessment. Curriculum-based assessments are designed to monitor the progress of students regularly, whereas standardized tests are given annually or semiannually to compare students to a norm. It is difficult to measure the progress of students on their IEP goals if they aren't monitored frequently. Answer A is incorrect because DIBELS is a common curriculum-based assessment that measures a student's abilities in reading. Answer B is incorrect because AIMSweb produces many curriculum-based assessment probes in the areas of reading, writing, and math. Answer C is incorrect because EasyCBM also assesses a student using curriculum-based assessment probes in many subjects.

73. D: When working with a student that is suspected to be a victim of abuse, it is not always beneficial to dig deep into what has occurred. Although some students may be open to sharing what has happened to them, others may not, and they might feel pressured. Many students with disabilities are victims of neglect and abuse, and they have a higher likelihood than their peers of being victims. Additionally, the role of a teacher or other staff member is usually to be a reporter of suspected abuse and neglect, not an investigator. Teachers and staff should remain anonymous, if possible, when reporting suspicion to maintain trust and a safe position. Answer A is incorrect because listening to the student to hear what he or she has to say may help calm them and help discover information. It is not advisable for teachers to look for more information when suspecting abuse or neglect, but any information that the student readily gives can be included in a report of suspicion to help with any subsequent investigations. Answer B is incorrect because reporting the incident to child services is mandatory. Answer C is incorrect because continuing to teach the class as usual will provide normalcy for the students and will help the student feel safe rather than in the spotlight. Victims of abuse often struggle with shame and guilt, so it is important for teachers to not draw unwanted attention to the student in normal environments like the classroom.

74. D: A word processor with voice output can help the student whose hearing impairment makes speech more difficult and less clear; the student with other communication deficits impeding expressive language and/or speech; the student with cognitive deficits impeding speech-language development; and, especially with prediction as well as voice output, the student with fine-motor skills deficits impeding typing. The touch screen (A) would benefit students with fine-motor skills deficits and cognitive deficits more than the others. Classroom amplification (B) would help the hard of hearing student, but not others. Large print/books on tape (C) would benefit students with visual impairments and/or cognitive deficits more than the others.

75. A: Whiteboards can be very helpful for students who struggle with writing to determine whether or not they understand the lesson. These students have an opportunity to show what they learned by writing it in a fun way. It is important to check and see if students are understanding the material in a way that doesn't feel like they are being assessed. Answer B is incorrect because self-assessments may not always provide the best information on how a student is performing. Answer C is incorrect because cooperative learning would likely be more appropriate for larger groups of students. Answer D is incorrect because flip charts might be better suited for younger students who need visuals to learn.

76. B: Asking students to create a play about the story as the teacher reads aloud would be the most effective strategy. This activity grounds the students in the story action as it is occurring. Acting it out ensures understanding; otherwise, the students will most likely stop the teacher and ask for clarification. Furthermore, by acting it out, students are incorporating understanding physically.

They will be more likely to retain the story and be able to comprehend the meanings incorporated in it.

77. B: Paraprofessionals provide instructional support to students with disabilities to ensure they have access to the curriculum. Paraprofessionals typically work under the guidance of special education teachers to make sure that students have the accommodations and modifications that they need. These professionals are instrumental in assisting the special education teacher and the general education teacher. Answer A is incorrect because teaching assistants can include a wide variety of people including student assistants or aides for general education classes. Answer C is incorrect because student teachers are typically students who are receiving on-the-job training to become teachers. Answer D is incorrect because behavior support professionals typically work on behavior deficits and not issues dealing with instructional assistance.

78. C: The most appropriate probe for a curriculum-based assessment in the area of written expression for a second grader would be to write a paragraph. Curriculum-based assessments are designed to see what a child is able to do by providing a challenge but giving him or her something that can be accomplished at a certain point. Writing paragraphs is something that students in second grade are likely working on or striving toward, which is why this probe would be beneficial for Jadon. Answer A is incorrect because second graders likely do not know how to write an essay yet. Answer B is incorrect because although spelling may be helpful, being able to compose sentences tends to be more valuable. Answer D is incorrect because writing one sentence likely does not provide quite enough information.

79. D: Students should be taught that writing is a process. By applying spelling patterns found in word families, the spelling of many words can be deduced. The other options are incorrect statements regarding teaching spelling. It is not true that knowing letter-sound association is enough alone to know how to spell. Simply knowing the origin of the root word, though potentially helpful, does not make instruction unnecessary. Drilling spelling exercises is often not the most effective long-term method of teaching spelling, as it can lead to frustration and a lack of interest on the part of the students.

80. C: The demonstration of learning should show whether or not a student met the daily objective. For students working on reading fluency, reading a short passage that is timed will show if they met the daily reading fluency objective. This is designed to be a quick assessment without any assistance from the teacher. Answer A is incorrect because reading a short story and answering questions may not be the best way to assess reading fluency. Answer B is incorrect because listening to a passage does not allow Brady to demonstrate his reading fluency ability. Answer D is incorrect because the demonstration of learning is designed to be an individual activity without assistance.

Practice Test #2

1. Which of the following does Vygotsky's term "scaffolding" refer to?

a. A structural framework that a teacher creates for a lesson
b. Support that is always present for a child with special needs
c. An organizational structure that guides social interactions
d. Support that is gradually withdrawn as independence grows

2. Ms. Winslow has a class with many students with learning disabilities (LD). She consistently calls her students' attention to features in their textbooks such as boldface headings, illustrations, tables, charts, indexes, and chapter summaries. Which is most accurate regarding this practice?

a. Doing this helps her students to organize what they read and learn.
b. She does this because her students don't read textbooks.
c. It enhances her presentation but does not really facilitate learning.
d. This helps her LD students but is a waste of time for other students.

3. Which of the following would be the best option in providing a fifth-grade student with a reading comprehension disability access to the curriculum in his reading class?

a. Modifying the content that the student reads
b. Accommodating the student by reading to him
c. Modifying the assignments that the student completes
d. Accommodating the student by giving him fewer questions

4. Which one of the following federal laws currently governs special education services in the United States?

a. Section 504 of the Rehabilitation Act
b. Individuals with Disabilities Education Act
c. Family Educational Rights and Privacy Act
d. Americans with Disabilities Act

5. Which of the following is an example of how Maslow's hierarchy of needs can be applied to motivate students?

a. Using fear to allow students to find security
b. Establishing structure to allow students to find self-actualization
c. Setting goals to allow students to build self-esteem
d. Providing food as a reward to fulfill basic needs

6. Shamus is an eighth-grade student with a specific learning disability in the area of written expression. Which of the following is the best example of a curriculum-based measure to monitor his progress in this area?

a. Giving him a story starter and counting his correct writing sequences
b. Giving him a list of spelling words to memorize and spell
c. Giving him a class period to construct an essay
d. Giving him a picture and asking him to write a sentence

7. Broca's aphasia is primarily:

a. An expressive language disorder
b. A disorder of receptive language
c. A disorder of both expressive and receptive language
d. A disorder of neither expressive nor receptive language

8. When selecting an intervention for a student who struggles with math problem solving, which of the following strategies would be least effective in improving the student's math skills?

a. Explicit instruction
b. Teaching vocabulary
c. Inquiry-based instruction
d. Graphic organizers

9. A student with ____________ has a great deal of difficulty with the mechanical act of writing. She drops her pencil, cannot form legible letters and cannot decode what she has written.

a. A nonverbal learning disorder
b. Dyslexia
c. Dyspraxia
d. Dysgraphia

10. Which of the following is the best example of how the results of an adaptive behavior scale can drive instruction?

a. To determine which problem behaviors the student engages in
b. To determine whether or not a student needs a behavior plan
c. To determine which independent living skills a student needs to work on
d. To determine how to adapt the curriculum to a student's needs

11. Rachel is a first-grade student who receives occupational therapy due to her struggles with handwriting. Which of the following sections of the IEP would be most likely to state the nature of this therapy?

a. Present levels
b. Accommodations
c. Service delivery
d. Prior written notice

12. Jacob is a ninth grader who receives special education services as a student with an emotional disturbance. In looking at the behavior rating scales that were given to his teachers and parents, the results were much different at home than they were at school. Which of the following is the most likely reason for this discrepancy?

a. Jacob's parents are not interested in using the rating scales properly.
b. Jacob's parents do not want the school to know his behaviors at home.
c. Jacob's teachers all see different behaviors at school.
d. Jacob's teachers and parents have different interpretations of the questions.

13. A teacher has shown a student with an intellectual disability a website that integrates music and video clips with a variety of educational games about a topic the student has shown interest in. The student is initially intimidated and fears interacting with the program might result in her breaking the computer. The teacher reassures her that she cannot harm the machine and shows the girl how to manipulate the mouse and keyboard. The teacher reminds the student what she already knows about the subject. As the student becomes more comfortable with the mouse, she focuses on the images and sounds, at times responding to the program conversationally, telling it what she knows about dinosaurs. The teacher is using the computer along with which teaching strategy?

a. Modular instruction
b. Scaffolding
c. Linking
d. Transmutation

14. Ms. Hardy finds that her elementary school students do not settle down enough after recess to focus on their math lesson. Which strategy would make best use of their instructional time?

a. Schedule their art class after recess and schedule the math lesson at another time.
b. Allow the students a time period after recess when they can settle down for math.
c. Cancel recess, telling the class they can have it if they settle down right away after.
d. Offer the students a coveted reward for getting perfect scores on their math tests.

15. What is true about educational strategies for facilitating communication with students from linguistically diverse backgrounds?

a. Giving class presentations is too stressful for ESL students
b. Peer-reading with lower-grade students will be humiliating
c. Conversational group projects will frustrate these students
d. Translating materials and interpreting speech will be useful

16. Researchers have found that to create a culturally responsive environment for enhancing reading comprehension, teachers should concentrate their endeavors on several elements, including teaching approaches and resource management. Which of the following is NOT another important element?

a. Positive classroom interactions
b. Curriculum and materials
c. Counseling and parent outreach
d. Teaching each class in the same manner regardless of the cultural makeup of the class

17. Which of the following is true of the procedural safeguards notice required by IDEA with regard to parents of students with disabilities?

a. Schools must provide the families a copy of their rights.
b. Schools must provide access to educational records.
c. Schools must provide a prior written notice.
d. Schools must provide an independent educational evaluation.

18. The desired outcomes a teacher places on their students can also be referred to as what?

a. Goals
b. Expectations
c. Rules
d. Procedures

19. A teacher suspects one of her kindergarteners has a learning disability in math. Why would the teacher suggest intervention to the child's concerned parents rather than assessment as the first step?

a. She wouldn't; assessment should precede intervention
b. She wouldn't; kindergarteners develop new skills at radically different rates. Suggesting either intervention or assessment at this point is premature. The teacher would more likely observe the child over a three month period to note her development before including the parents about her concern
c. Assessing a young child for learning disabilities often leads to an incorrect conclusion because a student must be taught the subject before it's possible to assess her understanding of it. Intervention teaches the child specific skills to correct her misconceptions. If the intervention fails, assessment is the next step
d. Assessment at this stage is unnecessary and wastes time and money. Since an assessment that resulted in a diagnosis of a learning disability would recommend intervention to correct it, it is more efficient to proceed directly to intervention

20. Which one of the following is the best example of cooperative learning when teaching a class that contains a mix of students with disabilities and the general education population?

a. Student-selected teams
b. Heterogeneous teams
c. Random teams
d. Homogeneous teams

21. When working with a group of students with emotional disturbances, which of the following would be the best example of a measurable objective?

a. Measuring how much a student's behavior has improved
b. Measuring the number of outbursts that a student has within a month
c. Measuring how well a student interacts with peers
d. Measuring how much work a student completes

22. Which of the following best describes when it would be appropriate to provide one-on-one in-class support to a fifth-grade student who receives special education services and has been demonstrating an inability to attend to his general education teachers?

a. As soon as the student demonstrates these behaviors
b. At the student's annual IEP meeting
c. After data have been collected and analyzed
d. When the student gets suspended from school

23. Dr. Gee reads the following sentence to a group of 5th graders: "The turquoise sky is reflected in the still lake. Fat white clouds floated on the lake's surface as though the water was really another sky. It was such a beautiful day. The students were to write the word "beautiful" in the blank. One student wrote 'pretty' instead. This suggests:

a. The student doesn't know the meaning of the word 'beautiful'.
b. The student is highly creative and believes he can substitute a word with a similar meaning.
c. The student did not know how to spell 'beautiful'.
d. The student did not hear what the teacher said. He heard 'pretty' instead of 'beautiful.'

24. Which of the following best describes alternate assessments and students that receive special education services?

a. Most students who receive special education services take alternate assessments.
b. Students who take alternate assessments do not receive high school diplomas.
c. Parents have the option to choose whether students take alternate assessments.
d. Alternate assessments must be based on grade-level standards.

25. Which of the following strategies would be most productive when differentiating the writing process for a student with a traumatic brain injury?

a. Allowing the student the use of a computer
b. Providing review sheets for exams
c. Reducing distractions on the student's desk
d. Slowing down the instructional pace in the class

26. Which of the following is the best example of an evidence-based assessment of a student's basic writing skills?

a. Test of Written Language (TOWL)
b. Informal observation by teacher
c. A classroom writing inventory
d. A rubric-based assessment

27. Which of the following is NOT an accurate statement regarding teaching reading skills to students with learning disabilities?

a. Using both visual and auditory input greatly increases comprehension.
b. Using both visual and auditory input greatly increases reading speed.
c. Using both visual and auditory input distracts and confuses students.
d. Using both visual and auditory input works better than either alone.

28. Richard is a sophomore in high school who is nonverbal. Which assistive technology devices would be MOST beneficial in allowing him to communicate effectively?

a. Audio players
b. FM listening systems
c. Schedule boards
d. Graphic organizers

Refer to the following for question 29:

A high school student struggles with applied math problems. He is given the following math problem. He selects a. 55 hours.

> **You are trying to travel from Point A to Point D and will need to change trains once. The first train travels from point A to point B in 3.5 hours. The same train travels from point B to point C in 2.75 hours. The second train leaves point C 1.25 hours after the first train arrives at point C. This train travels to point D in 45 minutes. The first train returns to point B in only 2.5 hours. How long does it take to travel from point A to point D?**
>
> a. 55 hours
> b. 97.60 hours
> c. 8.25 hours
> d. 19.75 hours

29. The teacher knows there are several ways to arrive at the correct answer. She also knows that if she explains them to the student, he will be able to understand where he made errors and see the relationships between various methods of solving applied math problems. The teacher should show the student how to:

a. Estimate the answer; think of the numbers in terms of minutes, and divide the answer by 60 to determine the number of hours and minutes; determine the percentage of an hour 45 minutes is, and write that number as .75; create a graph.
b. Estimate the answer; add the relevant numbers by removing the decimal points, then insert a decimal point in the answer; use a calculator to avoid problems in addition.
c. Re-think the numbers in terms of minutes only, and divide the answer by 60 to determine the number of hours and minutes; draw a picture of the train's progress in which the paper is divided into relative ratios; create a graph.
d. Estimate; create a graph; use a digital clock; add the relevant numbers together by removing the decimal points, then insert a decimal point in the answer.

30. When working with eighth-grade students on reading comprehension, what is the best strategy in ensuring that they are able to generalize these concepts across each of their classes?

a. Teaching them how to memorize certain parts of the text
b. Teaching them how to search for important information
c. Teaching them how to skim through the text
d. Teaching them how to reread passages

31. Which of the following is NOT true with regard to English learners receiving special education services?

a. There are no tests to definitively rule out learning disabilities.
b. They typically exhibit a disability in their native language first.
c. They must have adequate learning before a determination can be made.
d. Background knowledge can be a factor in the determination.

32. In a lesson plan, which of the following would NOT be included in the Instructional Procedures section?

a. Opening
b. Engagement
c. Assessment
d. Closure

33. One of the most important assessment tools for students with specific learning disabilities is a curriculum-based measure. Which of the following describes the MOST effective use of this kind of measure?

a. To determine whether or not a student is keeping up with his or her peers
b. To determine whether or not a student is making progress on his or her Individualized Education Program (IEP) goals
c. To determine whether or not a student is learning the curriculum
d. To determine whether or not a student has mastery of the curriculum

34. Mr. Stewart's students show good reading comprehension of any given paragraph in any chapter of their textbook, but they have trouble organizing, recalling, or applying the main points of a chapter. Which of the following is the simplest, most direct, and most efficient way to help?

a. Point out and explain the text's informational structure and features.
b. Create separate handouts with simplified organization of main points.
c. Identify, select, procure, duplicate, and distribute graphic organizers.
d. Create and deliver a slide show presentation for each text chapter.

35. Patrick is a third-grade student with IEP goals in math problem-solving and math calculations. What is the best instructional strategy to provide a spiraling curriculum?

a. Reviewing class material using similar instructional methods
b. Completing upcoming homework assignments in advance
c. Implementing both visual and auditory explanations of math content he learns in school
d. Increasing the complexity of the math work and problems gradually as he gains mastery

36. When teaching a small group of students with varying reading levels, what is the best strategy to ensure they are appropriately challenged?

a. Have the students read the same story, and give them comprehension questions at their ability levels.
b. Have the students read the same story, and have the more advanced students read aloud.
c. Have the students read different stories and work independently on their own questions.
d. Have the students read different stories, and have each student read their story aloud.

37. Which of the following functional curriculums would be most appropriate in supplementing the curriculum of a 10th-grade English class for students with autism?

a. Practice reading street signs
b. Practice reading textbooks
c. Practice reading computer terms
d. Practice reading grocery words

38. Which of the following is not likely to be included in both oral language achievement and written language achievement testing?

a. Mechanics
b. Narratives
c. Forming sentences
d. Both include all these

39. Which of the following intervention strategies would be most effective in assisting a student who struggles to learn vocabulary terms?

a. Providing the student with a multisensory model
b. Supplying visuals with the words
c. Creating frequent vocabulary quizzes
d. Allowing students to use a dictionary

40. Peter is a second-grade student with a specific learning disability in the area of writing and struggles to remember how to write his name. Which strategy would be best in helping him maintain that skill?

a. Asking him to practice writing his name for 30 minutes each day during a pullout group
b. Asking his teachers to help him practice writing his name throughout each day
c. Providing incentives and rewards each time he writes his name correctly
d. Giving him some extra writing materials to practice at home

41. Christopher is a student with concerns in the area of academics who scored in the below-average range on an academic achievement test. Which of the following disability categories would Christopher most likely be eligible for?

a. Speech or language impairment
b. Other health impairment
c. Specific learning disability
d. Cognitive disability

42. Approximately what percentage of the population is classified as intellectually disabled?

a. Less than 1%
b. 1 to 2%
c. 2 to 3%
d. 3 to 4%

43. Which is true about developmentally disabled students' transfer and maintenance of learning?

a. Instructional tasks and settings should resemble application tasks and settings.
b. Students should first acquire a skill, then gain fluency in it, and then transfer it.
c. Applying a skill should be done uniformly, without discriminating among cases.
d. Students should not practice fundamental skills until these become automatic.

44. A diabetic first grader is very pale, trembling and covered in a fine sweat. The teacher attempts to talk to the child, but the girl's response is confused and she seems highly irritable She is most likely experiencing:

a. Diabetic hypoglycemia.
b. Lack of sleep.
c. Hunger.
d. Diabetic hyperglycemia.

45. What steps are taken to identify specific skill deficits in math?

a. Standardized assessment tests, examining areas of weakness in student work to determine patterns, teacher observations, interviews with the student.
b. Standardized assessment tests, examining areas of weakness in student work to determine patterns, teacher observations, interviews with parents.
c. Teacher observations coupled with examining areas of weakness in student work are sufficient.
d. None of the above

46. Which of the following describes the purpose of an intelligence test?

a. To measure a student's ability to think abstractly
b. To measure a student's ability to understand spoken language
c. To measure a student's ability to convey ideas through oral language
d. To measure a student's ability to retain visual information

47. Alison is a fourth-grade student with a speech-language impairment due to stuttering. Which of the following strategies would be least effective in providing a supportive classroom environment?

a. Having her use prerecorded audio for presentations in which she has to speak
b. Having her collaborate with students that she is comfortable with
c. Having the teacher refrain from calling on her in class
d. Having her sit near the teacher at the front of class

48. Which of these is an advisable teacher strategy in organizing the learning environment to make it inclusive for students with disabilities as well as nondisabled students?

a. Decorating the classroom with as many bright colors, pictures, and furniture as possible
b. Storing books, manipulative objects, and other materials on high shelves to protect them
c. Creating an area as a "meeting spot" within the classroom where all of the students can gather
d. Placing students' desks far apart from one another to prevent students' distracting each other

49. How might a lesson introduction be most beneficial when teaching students with learning disabilities about math?

a. To provide students with additional information
b. To ensure that students understand the curriculum
c. To connect the learning from the previous lesson
d. To challenge the students to learn as much as possible

50. When does current federal legislation (IDEA 2004) require transition planning for students with disabilities to begin?

a. At age 18
b. At age 22
c. At age 14
d. At age 16

51. Regarding teaching strategies to improve reading fluency, teachers can encourage students to read independently by providing books with suitable difficulty levels that students find interesting. Which is true about these additional strategies?

a. Timed exercises should be avoided for creating undue pressure
b. Repetition is a very effective technique to build reading fluency
c. Readers' theatre is good for showing progress but not making it
d. Reading in pairs assists reading comprehension but not fluency

52. Which of the following is the goal of implementing a summative assessment?

a. To evaluate student learning
b. To determine the appropriate instruction
c. To monitor student learning
d. To compare students to a norm

53. Which of the following strategies would be LEAST effective in structuring an inclusive classroom environment?

a. Providing multisensory approaches to learning
b. Enforcing a rigidly structured routine
c. Developing clear rules and expectations
d. Using station learning opportunities

54. Which of the following best describes how daily learning objectives can be implemented to assist students who are working on adaptive skills?

a. To teach students to learn how to complete a new task
b. To teach students to improve reading ability
c. To teach students to learn about organization
d. To teach students to improve basic math skills

55. Which of the following best describes when it would be necessary for a teacher to create their own assessment?

a. When students do not have access to the curriculum
b. When testing students with intellectual disabilities
c. When providing accommodations to students
d. When the academic standards are modified

Refer to the following for question 56:

> A teacher is concerned about three of her students. While they are enthusiastic about writing, they do not always recognize letters, confusing *b*, *d*, and *p*, or *e* and *o*. They do, however, know which sounds go with certain letters when they are orally drilled. When they write, they appear to be attempting letter–sound associations.

"Now I'm writing *M*," the teacher heard one boy say as he scripted a large *N* in the upper right corner of his paper. He studied it for a moment and added, "Nope, it needs another leg." The student then wrote an *I* beside the *N*. "There," he said. "Now you are an *M*. I can write the word *man* because now I have *M*." The child then moved to the lower left corner of the paper. "M-A-N," he said to himself, slowly pronouncing each sound. "I already have that *M*. Here is where the rest of the word goes." He turned the paper sideways and wrote *N*.

The second child sang to herself as she gripped the crayon and scribbled lines here and there on her paper. Some of the lines resembled letters, but few actually were. Others were scribbles. As she "wrote," she seemed to be making up a story and seemed to believe she was writing the story down.

The third child didn't vocalize at all while he worked. He gripped the paper and carefully wrote the same letter over and over and over. Sometimes the letter was large, sometimes tiny. He turned the paper in every direction so that sometimes the letter was sideways or upside down. Sometimes he flipped it backward. "What are you writing?" the teacher asked him. "My name," the child told her. The teacher then realized the letter was, indeed, the first letter of his name. She gently told him he had done a fine job of writing the first letter of his name. Did he want her to help him write the rest of it? "Nope," he cheerfully told her, "it's all here." He pointed at one of the letters and "read" his full name. He pointed at another letter and again seemed to believe it represented all the sounds of his name.

56. In the above example, the emergent writers are demonstrating their understanding that letters symbolize predictable sounds, that words begin with an initial sound/letter, and that by "writing," they are empowering themselves by offering a reader access to their thoughts and ideas. The next three stages the emergent writers will pass through in order will most likely be:

a. Scripting the end-sound to a word (KT=cat), leaving space between words, writing from the top left to the top right of the page and top to bottom
b. Scripting the end-sound to a word (KT=cat), writing from the top left to the top right of the page and from top to bottom, separating the words from one another with a space between
c. Leaving space between the initial letters that represent words, writing from the top left to the top right of the page and from top to bottom, scripting the final sound of each word as well as the initial sound (KT=cat)
d. Drawing a picture beside each of the initial sounds to represent the entire word, scripting the end-sound to a word (KT=cat), scripting the interior sounds that compose the entire word (KAT=cat)

57. Lead teaching, learning centers/learning stations, resource services, team teaching, and consultation are all used in:

a. Innovative teaching
b. Strategic teaching
c. Collaborative teaching
d. Self-contained classrooms

58. Which of the following conditions would not typically be associated with a student with an emotional disturbance, according to IDEA?

a. An inability to learn that cannot be explained by intellectual, sensory, or health factors
b. A disability significantly affecting verbal communication and social interaction
c. An inability to build or maintain satisfactory interpersonal relationships
d. A tendency to develop fears associated with school problems

59. Joseph is a fourth-grade student being evaluated for special education services as a student with a specific learning disability in the area of math problem solving. Which of the following would be the best interpretation of his assessment results that show he is within one standard deviation of the mean in math problem solving?

a. Joseph would likely be determined eligible for special education services.
b. Joseph would likely need more testing in order to determine his eligibility.
c. Joseph would likely be determined ineligible for special education services.
d. Joseph would likely be determined eligible for a 504 Plan instead.

60. For which group of students would it be most appropriate to implement a functional curriculum at the elementary school level?

a. Students with intellectual disabilities
b. Students with specific learning disabilities
c. Students with speech or language impairments
d. Students with developmental delays

61. Mr. Hunt is a special education teacher with an elementary school class. He has one teacher's aide, one paraprofessional, and one parent volunteer, a mother, in his classroom. He uses peer tutoring methods as well. Three students—Marc, Fran, and Joe—have physical disabilities requiring assistance with snack time, bathroom breaks, and arts and crafts projects. One student, Clarence, likes to work alone on his math problems, but it is very important to him to have an adult check his work when he is done. Another student, Misty, is also very independent in her writing and art projects, but she needs the emotional support of periodic encouragement on her progress and praise for her results when she is done. Daisy and Carmela are similar in age and educational level and are friends, but Daisy excels in math and is below grade level in reading, while Carmela reads above her grade level but is below grade level in math. Which scenario is an example of the best use of Mr. Hunt's human resources in his classroom?

a. The paraprofessional assists Marc, Fran, and Joe with snacks, bathroom breaks, and arts and crafts projects; the teacher's aide checks Clarence's work and reports to Mr. Hunt so Mr. Hunt can explain Clarence's errors to him and assign additional exercises; the parent volunteer encourages and praises Misty; and Daisy and Carmela take turns helping each other in math and reading.
b. The paraprofessional checks Clarence's work, explains his errors, and assigns additional exercises; the parent volunteer takes Marc, Fran, and Joe to the bathroom; the teacher's aide helps with snacks; Daisy and Carmela take turns encouraging and praising Misty; and Mr. Hunt helps Marc, Fran, and Joe with arts and crafts projects.
c. Mr. Hunt takes Marc, Fran, and Joe to the bathroom; the parent volunteer checks Clarence's work, explains his errors, and assigns him additional exercises, and she helps with snacks; the paraprofessional helps Daisy with her reading and helps Marc, Fran, and Joe with arts and crafts; and the teacher's aide helps Carmela with her math.
d. Mr. Hunt encourages and praises Misty; Mr. Hunt helps Marc, Fran, and Joe with arts and crafts and takes them to the bathroom; the teacher's aide helps Marc, Fran, and Joe with snacks; the paraprofessional helps Carmela with math and Daisy with reading; and the parent volunteer checks Clarence's work, explains his errors, and assigns him additional exercises.

62. Academic achievement tests can be beneficial in evaluating students with academic struggles for special education and typically include subtests in many areas. Which subtest would NOT be included in one of these achievement tests?

a. Spelling
b. Numerical operations
c. Essay composition
d. Reasoning

63. A student with a disability takes online courses and struggles with communication and seeking help in social situations. Which of the following instructional strategies would be most effective in supporting the student in online instruction?

a. Supplementing online instruction with face-to-face instruction
b. Assisting the student in seeking support from the online teacher
c. Providing opportunities to demonstrate the knowledge learned online
d. Ensuring the student's accommodations are documented in the student's IEP

64. Cheyenne is an eighth-grade student with an OHI due to a heart condition, and she struggles with attendance. Which of the following would be the best example of a weekly objective in assisting Cheyenne in getting caught up?

a. Cheyenne will talk to each of her teachers at the beginning of each week.
b. Cheyenne will meet with her case manager to develop a plan for getting caught up.
c. Cheyenne will come in before school to talk to her teachers.
d. Cheyenne will complete all her missing assignments by the end of the week.

65. The left side of which lobe of the brain is most involved with mathematical calculations?

a. Parietal
b. Frontal
c. Occipital
d. Temporal

66. Which would be the best use for the results of a student's curriculum-based assessment?

a. To determine which grade level a student performs at
b. To determine a student's percentage in a class
c. To incorporate into an Individualized Education Program (IEP) to show progress
d. To incorporate in a student's school file

67. When teaching pull-out groups of elementary school students, which one of the following is a disadvantage to working with the students one on one rather than in small groups?

a. Students do not have access to their peers in one-on-one settings.
b. Students do not have access to the general education curriculum in one-on-one settings.
c. Students do not have access to their general education teachers in one-on-one settings.
d. Students do not have access to the special education curriculum in one-on-one settings.

68. Which of the following is a disadvantage to having special education teachers support classrooms rather than co-teach?

a. Special education teachers do not have as much time to plan.
b. Special education teachers are not as familiar with the content.
c. Special education teachers cannot differentiate instruction.
d. Special education teachers must collaborate with classroom teachers.

69. What would be the MOST effective instructional strategy in teaching a reading lesson to students with dyslexia?

a. Using a whole-word approach
b. Using multisensory strategies
c. Using modeling
d. Using graphic organizers

70. Which of the following is not an example of a strategy to improve students' generalization skills?

a. Assign field trips, role plays, etc., to apply new learning.
b. Provide multiple-choice games that include analogies.
c. Use a survey to identify students' favorite reinforcers.
d. Use math skills in banking, loans, paying for things, etc.

71. When transitioning from one subject to another and when she becomes anxious, a student always taps her front tooth 5 times then opens and closes her eyes 11 times before leaving her desk. The child most likely has:

a. Tic Disorder
b. Obsessive Compulsive Disorder
c. Anxiety Disorder
d. Depression

72. A special education teacher feels some of his strategies aren't effective. He asks a specialist to help him improve. The specialist suggests he:

a. Begin a journal in which he considers strategies he has used. Which seemed to work? Which didn't, and why?
b. Meet with the specialist to discuss the teacher's goals.
c. Permit the specialist to drop into his classroom unannounced to observe. This will prevent the teacher from unconsciously over-preparing.
d. Set up a video camera and record several student sessions to review. They can effectively collaborate at that time.

73. Andrea is a first-grade student with a developmental delay. Which formative assessment can be implemented to best monitor her progress throughout the school year?

a. Interviewing her each week
b. Giving her academic probes
c. Observing her in class
d. Monitoring her test scores

74. When teaching an eighth-grade class, which one of the following strategies in communicating with parents best promotes a safe classroom environment?

a. Sending home the list of class rules to the parents
b. Getting to know the background and interests of the parents
c. Ensuring that behavior issues are communicated to parents
d. Reporting positive student behavior to the parents

75. Madison is a third-grade student who receives special education services due to a hearing impairment. Which of the following special service providers would be LEAST likely to attend her reevaluation meeting?

a. Speech-language pathologist
b. Occupational therapist
c. School nurse
d. District audiologist

76. Which of the following is NOT a test to assess intelligence in students who do not use verbal communication (i.e., speech, writing)?

a. The Merrill-Palmer Scale
b. Raven's Progressive Matrices
c. Wechsler Adult Intelligence Scale
d. Leiter International Performance Scale-Revised

77. What statement is accurate regarding research findings about methods for teaching reading fluency?

a. Assisted reading approaches have been found highly effective for fluency.
b. Repeated reading and assisted reading approaches are mutually exclusive.
c. Assisted reading methods work equally well one-on-one and in regular classrooms.
d. Reading while listening is more efficient but unrelated to assisted reading.

78. Which of the following is true about stakeholder rights and an Independent Educational Evaluation (IEE)?

a. The testing is administered by someone who is not employed by the school district.
b. The IEP team must accept the results of the IEE.
c. The parents must pay for the IEE to be conducted.
d. The parents must explain the reason for the IEE.

79. What would be an example of effective feedback in a lesson plan for a third-grade class?

a. Selectively choosing students to call on
b. Immediately calling on a student after asking a question
c. Reinforcing student behavior
d. Providing corrective feedback the next day

80. Which classroom environment is most likely to support a student with attention-deficit/hyperactivity disorder (ADHD)?

a. Students with ADHD become bored easily, so a classroom with distinct areas for a multitude of activities will stimulate her. When she loses interest in one area, she can move to the next and continue learning.
b. Students with ADHD are highly aggressive and easily fall into depression. The teacher needs to provide a learning environment in which sharp objects such as scissors, tacks, or sharpened pencils are eliminated. This ensures greater safety for both student and teacher.
c. Students with ADHD are highly creative. A room with brightly colored mobiles, a multitude of visual and physical textures (such as striped rugs and fuzzy pillows) and plenty of art-based games will stimulate and encourage learning.
d. Students with ADHD are extremely sensitive to distractions. A learning environment in which visual and audio distractions have been eliminated is best. Low lighting, few posters, and a clean whiteboard help the student focus.

Answer Key and Explanations for Test #2

1. D: In Lev Vygotsky's sociocultural theory, the concept of scaffolding refers to support that is provided to learners (by parents, teachers, other adults, peers, etc.) when they need it to learn a task or skill, and which is gradually withdrawn as the learner becomes more able to perform that task or skill independently. It is a form of support for all learners, not just special needs children, and it is not always there (B), but is decreased little by little corresponding to the learner's progress. It is not a structural framework for a lesson (A) or for social interactions (C).

2. A: The most accurate answer is choice A: Doing this helps Ms. Winslow's students to organize what they read and learn from the textbooks. While many of us are familiar with students never reading their textbooks (B), this is not Ms. Winslow's main reason for her practice. The textbook items she regularly points out to her students are all specific organizational devices. Thus, answer C is incorrect: This practice may or may not enhance her presentation, but it does facilitate learning. Answer D—that this helps students with learning disabilities but is a waste of time for other students—is also incorrect, since all students can benefit from being reminded to use these features in their textbooks as aids to effective learning.

3. B: One of the best ways to provide access to a student with a disability in the area of reading comprehension is to provide accommodations. Reading the text to the student allows him to take in what he is reading and process it more clearly than if he was reading independently. Typically, it would not be as beneficial to modify or change the expectations of what the student completes. Answer A is incorrect because modifying what the student reads does not allow the student to access the curriculum that his peers are accessing. Answer C is incorrect because modifying the assignment may not give the student a chance to learn all of the material. Answer D is incorrect because giving a student fewer questions does not give the student access to all of the curriculum.

4. B: Although all of these laws play a role in supporting students with disabilities, the Individuals with Disabilities Education Act (IDEA) governs special education services. IDEA is responsible for ensuring that students with disabilities are given their rights and supports that meet their needs. IDEA is instrumental in protecting not only students with disabilities but also teachers and other providers that work with students with disabilities. Answer A is incorrect because Section 504 is a civil rights act that protects everyone with disabilities, not just students. Answer C is incorrect because the Family Educational Rights and Privacy Act protects the confidentiality of students' educational records and personal information. Answer D is incorrect because the Americans with Disabilities Act is a civil rights law that prohibits discrimination against individuals with disabilities. It is not related to special education services.

5. C: Setting goals for students in order to give them something to strive for and providing an opportunity for success can build self-esteem. Without this self-esteem, students will lack confidence and not be able to accomplish as much. According to Maslow's hierarchy of needs, human needs are arranged in a hierarchy and can provide value in seeking to motivate students. Answer A is incorrect because using fear is not a tactic that will allow students to find security. Answer B is incorrect because establishing structure, although it may be beneficial to some students, will likely not help those students find self-actualization unless creativity is allowed. Answer D is incorrect because providing food is considered a basic physiological need that should not be used as a conditional reward.

6. A: Giving a student like Shamus a story starter and counting his correct writing sequences is one of the most beneficial curriculum-based assessments. This assessment focuses on many areas including spelling, punctuation, and content of the writing. Students that struggle with writing will often need practice writing short stories such as these, and it is easy to monitor their progress. Answer B is incorrect because simply giving him a list of spelling words only allows the teacher to focus on one area, spelling. Answer C is incorrect because curriculum-based assessments are not designed to take an entire class period. Answer D is incorrect because giving him a picture to write about might be more appropriate for a younger student.

7. A: Broca's aphasia is primarily an expressive language disorder. It causes difficulty with facets of expressive language, including processes involving recall of specific words, constructing sentences with correct syntax, and other aspects of speaking and writing. It is not a disorder of receptive language (B), which affects comprehension rather than production, nor of both types (C). Since it is a disorder of expressive language, answer D, neither type, is incorrect.

8. C: Although inquiry-based instruction can be beneficial for many students when learning math, many students that struggle will likely need more instruction and steps on how to solve problems. Inquiry-based instruction relies on the students to ask the questions, which can be difficult for struggling students. Students who struggle with math problem solving often struggle with vocabulary and executive functioning. Answer A is incorrect because explicit instruction can be beneficial so that students know exactly how to solve the problems. Answer B is incorrect because vocabulary development is beneficial to students who struggle with math problem solving and do not understand certain terminology. Answer D is incorrect because graphic organizers can help provide organizational support to students in solving math problems.

9. D: Dysgraphia. Dysgraphic individuals cannot manage the physical act of writing. While many dysgraphics are highly intelligent and able to express themselves cogently, they have extreme difficulty holding a writing implement and shaping letters.

10. C: Adaptive behavior scales are used to determine which independent living skills a student has and what the student may need to work on. These assessments are typically used for students with intellectual disabilities or other severe disabilities to understand what instruction needs to be implemented. These tests typically consist of an evaluation of a student's social skills, daily living skills, communication skills, and other skills that the student will need after high school. Answer A is incorrect because the primary purpose of these scales is to identify skill deficits, not to diagnose behavior problems. Answer B is incorrect because the adaptive behavior scale is not used to determine whether or not a student needs a behavior plan. Answer D is incorrect because while adaptive behavior scales can inform curriculum, answer C is more specific about what needs to be taught (independent living skills).

11. C: The service delivery section of the IEP describes what services a student will be provided and the nature of those services. This may include the amount of time that a student receives these services for and who will provide the services. This section is crucial in describing the services that must be provided and ensuring that the services are provided for an allotted amount of time. Answer A is incorrect because the present levels section describes how a student is currently performing. Answer B is incorrect because the accommodations section of the IEP describes the accommodations that the student will be provided in the general education setting. Answer D is incorrect because a prior written notice describes the changes that the school proposes or refuses to a student's identification, evaluation, educational placement, or services.

12. D: Because the setting is different, it is expected that Jacob's behavior may look different to different people. It is also possible that the teachers and parents have different interpretations of the questions. Answer A is incorrect because there is nothing to indicate a lack of interest on the part of Jacob's parents. Answer B is not as likely as answer D because parents aren't likely to provide incorrect answers on purpose. Answer C is incorrect because there is nothing in the stem to suggest that the teachers differ in their results.

13. B: Scaffolding is an umbrella teaching approach that offers a multitude of supports. Scaffolding includes prior knowledge, mnemonic devices, modeling, graphs, charts, graphic organizers, and information needed prior to starting the lesson such as vocabulary or mathematical formulas.

14. A: The strategy to make best use of instructional time is for Ms. Hardy to (A) schedule their art class, which is more active than a math lesson and which the children enjoy, following recess when their elevated moods are more amenable to this activity. Allowing time to settle down (B) does not make the best use of instructional time, as lesson time is lost while they are simply calming down. (This could be beneficial but is a luxury not feasible in most schools.) Canceling recess (C) is punitive. Research finds that students with the kinds of academic and/or behavioral deficits more likely to be punished are the very students who most need recess. It affords physical activity as well as cognitive, academic, and social benefits. Offering recess as a reward in advance of settling down instead of after that desired behavior would not be effective, as positive reinforcement should immediately follow desired behavior, not precede it. The children are likely to be unable to comply. Offering a reward for perfect math test scores (D) misses the point: The children's problem is not lack of interest or motivation for math, but rather inability to transition from the active recess situation to the quieter, more focused math activity. The transition to a more active lesson like art is likely to be easier for them.

15. D: Translating educational materials and interpreting speech into students' native languages helps promote communication. Offering ESL students opportunities to give class presentations (not forcing them) is not too stressful (A) for many; those who have learned enough English can be eager to show what they have learned, building self-esteem. Similarly, peer-reading with lower-grade students is not necessarily humiliating (B); ESL students get to read at levels more appropriate to their English levels and can benefit by helping younger students in other ways (e.g., sharing more mature social skills, life experiences, and another language) as they improve their English reading with less pressure to meet grade-level expectations prematurely. Conversational group projects are useful for further English language development. Students are likely to find these interactions more fun and interesting than frustrating (C); all participants will likely learn something of languages and cultures other than their own.

16. D: By promoting positive classroom interactions, teachers can improve students' confidence, willingness to participate, and engagement in instruction. By paying attention to the curriculum and materials they use, teachers can facilitate learning by making it more meaningful to students. For example, they can provide reading material with which students can identify personally through themes they recognize, validating their cultural identity. Counseling provides students with the opportunity to express wants, needs, and feelings, even as it allows teachers to help students cope with these, gain insights, and adjust to environmental differences. Parent outreach gets families involved in students' education and provides teachers with valuable information about students' learning problems, strengths, interests, and strategies that have and have not worked at home and/or in previous schools. Because cultural responsiveness involves adapting classroom instruction to the cultural experiences and knowledge of the students in class, teaching in the same manner regardless of cultural makeup is the antithesis of cultural responsiveness.

17. A: The family of students who receive special education services must be provided a copy of their procedural safeguard rights, according to IDEA. These safeguards allow the family to know and understand what they can do if they have questions or concerns about the services that their family member may be receiving. These are important in establishing the ground rules of special education laws and services. Answer B is incorrect in this context because the question is asking specifically about what the procedural safeguards notice itself does (it requires the school to give parents a written explanation of their rights). While IDEA (and FERPA) give parents the right to access educational records, that is a substantive procedural safeguard, not the defining feature of the notice. Answer C is incorrect because although schools must provide prior written notice, this is separate from the procedural safeguard rights. Answer D is incorrect because the school is not required to provide an independent educational evaluation.

18. B: A teacher's expectations are the desired result of their goals. On the other hand, goals are the means to obtaining the outcomes. For example, a goal may be to complete lesson one by the end of week one. This goal will determine the activities the teacher plans for that week. The teacher will also have the expectation that her student will complete and understand the lesson. Rules and procedures typically refer to acceptable behavior in the classroom. Effective classroom management will detail the rules of the classroom as well as the process to follow those rules. Taken together, well-thought-out goals, expectations, rules, and procedures will yield a well-run classroom.

19. C: Assessing a young child for learning disabilities often leads to an incorrect conclusion because a student must be taught the subject before it is possible to assess her understanding of it. Intervention teaches the child specific skills to correct her misconceptions. If the intervention fails, assessment is the next step. Because formal diagnoses of specific learning disabilities can be less reliable at very young ages, teachers typically begin with classroom interventions and progress monitoring, referring for a formal evaluation if concerns persist over time.

20. B: In order to allow for collaboration among students with and without disabilities, heterogeneous teams are likely to be most productive. In these groups, the teacher selects which students are in which groups in order to create a balance of ability levels among the students. This allows students with disabilities to have some success in working with students they may not always have the opportunity to work with. Answer A is incorrect because student-selected teams may leave some students with disabilities feeling left out because they were not chosen for a group. Answer C is incorrect because random teams may create an imbalance between students with and without disabilities in the class. Answer D is incorrect because homogeneous teams would group students based on ability, which would likely not make for the best balance in the class.

21. B: Although all of these objectives may be beneficial, they cannot all necessarily be measured. The number of outbursts a student has over a given time period is something that can be calculated and measured. Measurable objectives should also be realistic for a student to achieve over a certain time period. Answer A is incorrect because it is impossible to measure how much a student's behavior improves without quantifiable data. Answer C is incorrect because it is difficult to measure social interactions, and no time period is given. Answer D is incorrect because although it is possible to measure how much work a student completes, no time period is given. This makes Answer B a better option.

22. C: In order to understand why student behaviors have increased or declined, it is important to collect data before making major changes. Providing support to a student one on one is a significant change to the instruction that the student receives, so it should not be implemented until data have been collected on the student. These data might include what times of the day these behaviors arise or what kind of interactions may be involved with certain behaviors. Answer A is incorrect because the behavior may simply be a short-term situation in which the student does not display them consistently. Answer B is incorrect because although it may be a good thing to discuss at the annual IEP meeting, these do not always fall at the same time that changes need to be implemented. Answer D is incorrect because student suspensions do not necessarily dictate the level of support that a student receives in a class.

23. C: The student did not know how to spell 'beautiful'. It is doubtful the student heard "pretty" instead of beautiful since the two sound nothing alike. It is equally unlikely he doesn't know the meaning of the word 'beautiful' since his substitution, 'pretty', is a synonym for beautiful. It is likely this child is creative, but that alone wouldn't be sufficient reason to replace one word with another. The most logical answer is that he simply didn't know how to spell 'beautiful'. He does know that some words mean almost the same thing, and since he already knew how to spell 'pretty', he incorrectly believed a synonym would be acceptable.

24. D: Alternate assessments must be based on grade-level standards for students. Alternate assessments are created for students who are unable to participate in general assessments with accommodations. Answer A is incorrect because most students who receive special education services take the general assessment. Answer B is incorrect because although many students who take the alternate test do not receive a high school diploma, this is not always the case. Answer C is incorrect because the decision about alternate testing is typically up to the IEP team based on the needs of the student.

25. A: Although all of these choices can be beneficial to students with traumatic brain injuries, allowing them the use of a computer is most productive with regard to writing. The use of a computer can help alleviate some of the stress and anxiety associated with the written product. Students with traumatic brain injuries often struggle with stress and anxiety, and using a computer can help with this. Answer B is incorrect because providing review sheets for an exam would be beneficial for studying for a test but not particularly helpful for writing during a writing lesson. Answer C would not be as directly helpful with writing as a computer. Answer D is incorrect because slowing down the instructional pace for the whole class is not an example of differentiation, and it isn't likely to help considerably with writing.

26. A: The TOWL is the best example of an evidence-based assessment of a student's basic writing skills because its results are norm-referenced and supported by experimental research results. The other choices are all equally effective methods of assessing basic student writing. While they can be informed by research, they rely on individual teacher methods and/or individual student writing samples, and they are not typically proven by evidence from research studies and do not compare student results to those of normative student sample groups.

27. C: It is incorrect that using both visual and auditory input (C) distracts or confuses students with learning disabilities. The information is reinforced for them when presented in both sensory modalities. Special educators find that students' reading comprehension can improve dramatically when spoken language is presented along with printed language (A). They also find that students with reading learning disabilities, who typically read slowly and laboriously, can increase their reading speed just as dramatically when the auditory version is added to the visual (B). Therefore, it is correct that using visual and auditory input together is more effective than either sensory modality alone (D).

28. C: Schedule boards and communication boards allow people to communicate what their daily schedule is going to be and anything else they may need to communicate. Answer A is incorrect because audio players are for students who struggle with reading. Answer B is incorrect because listening systems are to help reduce background noise and improve sound clarity. Answer D is incorrect because graphic organizers tend to be for those students who struggle with executive functioning.

29. A: Choice A properly outlines how the student could find the correct answer. The other options include methods that could overcomplicate the calculation or that would not be helpful.

30. B: Although each of these can be helpful in improving reading comprehension abilities, being able to search for important information can help in any subject matter. Answer A is incorrect because students who struggle with reading comprehension will also likely struggle to memorize. Answer C is incorrect because, although skimming can help students get a general sense of a text, by itself it does not ensure they can consistently identify and use the most important information across subjects. Answer D is incorrect because rereading is a helpful repair strategy, but without explicitly teaching students how to recognize and focus on key information, rereading alone may not support generalization across all classes.

31. B: Students who are English learners do not necessarily exhibit a learning disability in their native language before English. Sometimes the deficit is apparent in one language and not the other, and many times it is apparent in both. It is important to understand the history of each student when making the determination. Answer A is incorrect because there is not one single test that predicts special education eligibility for English learners. Answer C is incorrect because it is imperative that these students receive proper learning before they can be properly evaluated. Answer D is incorrect because where a student was raised and what they know can also be deciding factors.

32. C: Three components of an effective lesson plan included under Instructional Procedures are Opening (A), i.e., getting students interested, activating their existing knowledge, and connecting the new material to it; Engagement (B), i.e., facilitating and monitoring active and reflective student learning and discourse and asking specific questions to help students take risks and develop deeper understanding; and Closure (D), i.e., highlighting main lesson points for student comprehension, giving students opportunities to share their comprehension, and asking questions to obtain meaningful student feedback. Assessment (C) is not an instructional procedure but a separate section covering how you evaluate student learning and how it aligns with lesson objectives.

33. B: Curriculum-based measures are used in special education as quick, frequent assessments to determine whether or not students are making sufficient progress on their IEP goals. If a student with a specific learning disability falls behind on one of his or her IEP goals, the IEP team can review and implement measures to help the student before he or she falls too far behind. Choice A is incorrect because it refers to a type of norm-referenced test, where a student's scores are compared to similar students' scores. Choice C is incorrect because the most effective use of curriculum-based measures for a student with a specific learning ability is monitoring IEP progress, not general curriculum progress. Choice D is incorrect because curriculum-based measures do not always translate to official grades, as they are simply a progress-marking tool.

34. A: Textbooks incorporate informational structure, such as presenting items in chronological order, comparisons and contrasts, and pointing out causal relationships. They also use informational features such as boldface type, sub-headings, bullet points, review questions, glossaries, an index, etc., to assist students in organizing, remembering, and applying information, even though many students may not use them. The simplest, most direct, and most efficient way that Mr. Stewart can help his students is to point these out and explain how to use them. Creating separate handouts (B) takes more time and work and may duplicate what the text already does. Graphic organizers (C) are excellent aids, especially for students who learn more visually than verbally, but they also involve more work than using the text. Mr. Stewart's students have good reading comprehension but cannot organize whole chapters. A slide show is an excellent supplement to the text but should not replace an explanation of the text's informational aids.

35. D: A spiraling curriculum involves revisiting key concepts throughout instruction in increasing complexity and depth, building upon previous learning. Reviewing material in the same way as it was initially taught (A) doesn't involve progression. Completing homework in advance (B) does not involve revisiting content with increased complexity. While implementing visual and auditory explanations (C) might be useful, it is not an example of spiraling curriculum.

36. C: When working with students with varying levels in the area of reading, it is important to challenge each student appropriately while also making good use of the time. Having the students work independently on their own stories and questions accomplishes both of these. Answer A is incorrect because some of the students may not be appropriately challenged if they all read the same story. Answer B is incorrect because the students who struggle more may not get enough practice. Answer D is incorrect because this may not be the most appropriate use of time.

37. D: Although all of these choices can be beneficial in helping these students with tasks they may need after high school, grocery story reading a high-priority functional literacy target because nearly all students will shop for food. While reading street signs, textbooks, and computer-related text can be important depending on individual goals and should not be dismissed outright, these students are likely to visit grocery stores frequently and will need to be able to read certain words in order to make purchases. Functional curriculum can help students with skills they will need when they are finished with school. Answer A is incorrect because although reading street signs can help these students, they may or may not experience driving. Answer B is incorrect because reading textbooks will likely not be a skill they will need. Answer C is incorrect because even though these students will likely use computers throughout their life, this is something that can be self-taught or practiced at home.

38. A: Mechanics (A) are likely to be included in written language achievement testing but not in oral language achievement testing. Spelling and punctuation cannot be assessed in speech, and other mechanics are never as correct in speech as in writing, even by those without any learning disabilities. Narratives (B) are likely to be included in both types of testing, as they demonstrate the ability to sequence events chronologically, to retain and retrieve information, to express that information in language, to tell a story, and to recognize narrative elements such as characters, actions, and settings. While elements such as themes and styles are more applicable to written language, oral narratives are valid (and predate written narratives historically) for assessing the aforementioned abilities. If a student has difficulties or irregularities specifically with forming sentences (C), rather than with either oral or written expression, this is equally likely to show up in spoken or written language when sentence formation is tested.

39. B: Students tend to remember vocabulary words when they have some kind of visual to associate with the word. Many students that struggle with vocabulary words often need a lot of practice in understanding these new words, so giving them multiple methods to learn the words is beneficial. Simply telling the students what words to memorize often does not work with students with disabilities that struggle with vocabulary. Answer A is incorrect because providing a multisensory model may be helpful for some students but is not the most effective method of learning new vocabulary. Answer C is incorrect because additional vocabulary quizzes might become too overwhelming for some students. Answer D is incorrect because although a dictionary can help learn the term at first, this strategy will not likely be effective in the long term.

40. B: The best way for students to maintain a skill that they struggle to work on is to continue to work on that skill across subjects and at different times throughout the day. Answer A is incorrect because just having him work on it once a day will likely not give him enough opportunities to practice it no matter how long he practices it. Answer C is incorrect; although these incentives may work at first, it is likely not going to help him long term in remembering to write his name. Answer D is incorrect because having him complete extra homework will likely make him resent writing and not want to do it.

41. C: Students who score in the below-average range on achievement tests with no other concerns will typically fall under the "specific learning disability" category. Students with specific learning disabilities have deficits in the areas of reading, writing, and math. It is important to understand the results of assessments in order to appropriately place students and provide services that the student will need. Answer A is incorrect because students with trouble in speech or communication would take a test specific to those needs. Answer B is incorrect because students who receive services under the other health impairment category will have a health impairment that impacts their access to education. Answer D is incorrect because a cognitive disability is not one of the disability categories under the Individuals with Disabilities Education Act.

42. C: Approximately 2 to 3% of the population is classified as intellectually disabled, and there are approximately 7 million intellectually disabled individuals in the United States.

43. A: Educators and researchers working with DD students find similarities between tasks and settings during both instruction and application facilitate transfer. They also find the traditional three-stage hierarchy of skill acquisition, fluency, and transfer (B) is NOT as effective as supporting transfer from the beginning of instruction. Another factor facilitating transfer is the student's ability to discriminate (C) when or when NOT to apply a learned skill. Transfer and maintenance are additionally supported by practicing relevant basic skills until these become automatic (D): students must be fluent in foundations to attain higher learning levels.

44. A: Diabetic hypoglycemia. Diabetic hypoglycemia, also known as insulin reaction, occurs when blood sugar falls to a very low level. It is important to treat it quickly or the diabetic could faint, in which case an injection of glucagon is administered.

45. A: Standardized assessment tests, examining areas of weakness in student work to determine patterns, teacher observations, and interviews with the student are the typical steps taken to identify specific skill deficits in math. After this, the teacher should be well-prepared to plan instruction.

46. A: The purpose of an intelligence test is to measure a student's ability to reason and solve problems, which includes thinking abstractly. Intelligence tests can provide valuable information in deciphering the reasons that a student may struggle in particular areas. These tests can be beneficial for students of all grades and disabilities for gathering information. Answer B is incorrect because measuring a student's spoken language abilities would be considered a processing assessment. Answer C is incorrect because measuring a student's ability to convey ideas through oral language would be considered a communication assessment. Answer D is incorrect because visual information assessments would typically fall under the visual-spatial assessment categories.

47. C: Although it may be beneficial to allow her to not be called on in class, this may also cause her to be self-conscious. She might not be comfortable speaking in front of the class, but this strategy may cause her to feel ignored compared to other students. It is important to have a conversation with students like Alison to determine what they are comfortable with and how they can be best supported. Answer A is incorrect because allowing her to use prerecorded audio for presentations might make her feel less stress about talking in front of the class. Answer B is incorrect because giving her the opportunity to collaborate with peers that she knows can help her be supported in the class. Answer D is incorrect because allowing her to sit in front of the class might make it easier to access the teacher.

48. C: Expert educators recommend creating a "meeting" area big enough for all students in the class to gather for participating in large group activities, engaging in discussions, and developing their social skills. Too many bright colors and clutter (A) can cause sensory overload and/or distractions for disabled (and nondisabled) students. Storing class materials on high shelves (B) makes them inaccessible to non-ambulatory, physically disabled, and smaller students. Teachers also recommend placing students' desks in small groups rather than far apart (D): grouping desks gives students more opportunities for learning collaboration, cooperation, and discussion.

49. C: For students with learning disabilities in the area of math, it is important to break down their learning to demonstrate how everything fits together. If they struggled with the previous lesson, they may need some additional instruction before they can move on to the next lesson. It is important that they are instructed at a speed and level that meet their needs and ensure that there is a smooth transition between topics. Answer A is incorrect because simply providing students with learning disabilities with more information may overwhelm them. Answer B is incorrect because ensuring that they understand the curriculum will likely occur as the lesson is being taught and not before. Answer D is incorrect because it may not be appropriate to challenge these students while learning is still occurring.

50. D: The 1997 version of IDEA required transition planning to begin when the student was 14 years old (C). The 2004 reauthorization of this law changed the age to 16. Some students with disabilities, such as those with autism spectrum disorders, often need extended time periods for transition planning, so many special educators still advocate beginning at age 14. Some individual states also specify age 14. The later age in the current reauthorization may reflect considerations related to developmental levels. Some students with disabilities need more time to complete secondary education. However, others will graduate at age 18 (A), so this can be too late for transition planning. (Under IDEA, legal rights to transition planning and services generally transfer from parents to students when students reach the age of majority as defined by state law, which is often 18.) Students with disabilities have the legal right to attend school until they graduate or reach the age of 22 (B), so transition planning must start before this.

51. B: The only true choice is (B): Repetition is very effective for building reading fluency. The teacher can have the student read a passage aloud repeatedly until s/he achieves the desired fluency, and then progress to a harder selection. Timing this exercise also promotes fluency, which includes speed as well as accuracy; therefore (A) is incorrect: Timed exercises should not be avoided in remediating fluency problems. Teachers can also use timing by giving students "speed drills" for individual words. A non-timed exercise can be having a student repeatedly read a familiar book out loud, giving feedback and direction as needed. Another technique is a readers' theatre; it is not true that this is good for showing progress but not making progress (C). The practice and feedback component of this exercise aids with improvement, even as it showcases progress in fluency. It is not true that reading in pairs increases comprehension but not fluency (D); partner/paired reading promotes both.

52. A: The goal of a summative assessment is to evaluate what a student has learned over a specific topic or topics. Summative assessments are typically graded and may include some kind of a test or paper that the students are responsible for. Summative assessments can be valuable for students with disabilities for many reasons, including assessing a student's progress on IEP goals or whether or not a student's supports have been beneficial. Answer B is incorrect because determining appropriate instruction would be considered a diagnostic assessment. Answer C is incorrect because monitoring student learning would be considered a formative assessment. Answer D is incorrect because comparing students to a norm would be considered a norm-referenced or standardized assessment.

53. B: Although some students may thrive in a structured routine, it is important for the teacher to be open to change and be flexible. It is possible that lesson plans or teaching strategies don't go as planned, so it is important for the teacher to be able to change the routine when needed. An overly rigid or structured routine could force the teacher and class into an ineffective plan. Students with disabilities will especially need flexibility from the teacher on a daily basis. Answer A is incorrect because every student in the class can benefit from a multisensory approach. Answer C is incorrect because developing clear rules and expectations allows the students to understand what they can and cannot do in the class. Answer D is incorrect because station learning can allow students to work with peers and learn using a variety of techniques.

54. A: Adaptive skills are skills that people use every day in order to function at home, school, or work. There are many skills in caring for oneself and accessing the community that are important to practice and complete in order to demonstrate understanding. When teaching these skills, it is important to provide opportunities to practice these tasks to determine what students have mastered and what skills need additional work. Answer B is incorrect because although improving reading ability is important, it would not likely help students in learning everyday skills to function. It is more of an academic skill. Answer C is incorrect because learning about organization is not typically a skill that is practiced in isolation when considering adaptive skills. Answer D is incorrect because although basic math skills are also important skills, they would not be the most effective skill to teach when working on a student's adaptive skills.

55. D: Although all of these choices may provide instances to change the test or the format of the test, it is likely most beneficial to create a new test when the standards are modified. When students are unable to access the regular academic standards, it is often necessary to create a new assessment to meet the needs of these students and assess what they know. Although the majority of students can access these regular standards with accommodations or modifications, some students need to work with modified standards due to their disability. Answer A is incorrect because students who do not have access to the curriculum would likely not be assessed at all. Answer B is incorrect because students with intellectual disabilities may or may not be able to access the standards with accommodations or modifications. Answer C is incorrect because accommodated tests typically do not involve a new test being created.

56. A: The next three stages are scripting the end-sound to a word (KT=cat), leaving space between words, and writing from the top left to the top right of the page and from top to bottom. Each of these steps is progressively more abstract. Scripting the end-sound to a word helps a young writer recognize that words have beginnings and endings. This naturally leads to the willingness to separate words with white space so that they stand as individual entities. Once this step is reached, the child realizes that in English, writing progresses from left to right and from the top of the page to the bottom.

57. C: Classrooms with a lead teacher often include a specialized teacher to listen to the lesson and work with special needs children. Other methods of collaborative teaching are learning centers or stations in which collaborating teachers are responsible for different areas, assigning special needs students into a resource room, and team teaching and/or consultation by the special education teacher to the classroom teacher.

58. B: A disability that significantly affects verbal communication and social interaction falls under the "autism spectrum disorder disability" category. An emotional disturbance is a condition with certain characteristics that occur over a period of time and affects a child's educational performance. According to IDEA, students that display characteristics of autism will typically fall under the autism spectrum disorder category. Answer A is incorrect because students with emotional disturbances often have an inability to learn that cannot be explained by these factors. Answer C is incorrect because these students often have a difficult time building relationships. Answer D is incorrect because fears associated with school are also common for students with an emotional disturbance.

59. C: When students fall within one standard deviation of the mean, this is most often considered in the average range, and a student would not be eligible. Students being evaluated for a specific learning disability must have a score that is considered statistically significant in order to be eligible. It is important to understand where one standard deviation falls in order to determine where the student scores. Answer A is incorrect because the student would likely not be eligible unless they were outside one standard deviation. Answer B is incorrect because although it is possible that more testing could be considered, this score shows that the student is within the average range. Answer D is incorrect because there is likely not enough information to determine whether or not a 504 Plan would be appropriate for Joseph.

60. A: Although functional curriculum can be implemented for students of any age or disability, it is most often taught to students with intellectual disabilities. Functional curriculum focuses on life skills and other daily living skills that students will need after high school. It may be appropriate for certain students to start working on some of these skills as early as the elementary school level. Answer B is incorrect because students with specific learning disabilities likely would not access this curriculum until high school. Answer C is incorrect because students with speech or language impairments are not likely to need this curriculum to supplement their knowledge. Answer D is incorrect because students with developmental delays may or may not access this curriculum later on, but the elementary school age tends to be early for most students.

61. A: The paraprofessional can assist with physical needs. The aide can check Clarence's work but should refer re-teaching and assignment of exercises to Mr. Hunt. The parent volunteer is a good choice to give Misty emotional support. Daisy and Carmela are the best choices for peer tutoring since they are very alike in age and grade level but are opposites when it comes to strengths and weaknesses in math and reading. Therefore, option A is correct.

The paraprofessional can check Clarence's work but should not explain or assign exercises. The teacher should do these things. The parent volunteer may or may not be comfortable taking children other than her own to the bathroom. Misty may appreciate the peer approval implicit in receiving emotional support from Daisy and Carmela, but she may also prefer adult approval. Since Daisy and Carmela's strengths and weaknesses are so opposite and their other characteristics are so similar, their helping each other is a more directly beneficial use of peer tutoring. If both girls are busy supporting Misty, they will have less time and attention to help each other and make their own progress. Although the teacher can give physical help with arts and crafts when he is the only adult in the class, since others are present who can help with this, he can do more teaching. Therefore, option B is incorrect.

As the teacher, Mr. Hunt should not be taking students to the bathroom while the volunteer, the paraprofessional, and the aide do his teaching tasks. Therefore, option C is incorrect.

In option D, Mr. Hunt is doing too many things considering how many helpers he has in his room. He is supporting Misty, helping the physically disabled students with arts and crafts, and also taking them to the bathroom. At the same time, the paraprofessional and the volunteer are doing his teaching tasks. Therefore, option D is incorrect.

62. D: Although reasoning can be an important skill to assess, this would typically be associated with an IQ test rather than an academic achievement test. Answer A is incorrect because spelling is one of the subtests commonly found in an achievement test. Answer B is incorrect because numerical operations are found in most achievement tests. Answer C is incorrect because an essay composition portion of the test is common for older students taking achievement tests.

63. B: Assisting the student in seeking support from the online teacher would likely be the most helpful for the student out of the options listed. Students who take online classes often struggle to understand how to seek help or who to contact if they need it. The question notes that the student often has trouble seeking help, so this would be a good first step.

The question also notes that the student struggles with communication in social situations, so face-to-face instruction likely would not be helpful. Option C focuses on assessment instead of instructional access. Option D focuses on administrative responsibility, which would not directly help the student access online instruction.

64. B: Although it may be difficult to plan when she will be absent from school, it would be beneficial to Cheyenne to have someone such as her case manager support her in this task. Making up work on a regular basis can be difficult to do for anyone, especially an eighth grader with a disability. The case manager can help Cheyenne come up with a plan for working with her teachers and getting her assignments in. Answer A is incorrect because although it may be helpful to have Cheyenne talk to her teachers, it may be an overwhelming task. Answer C is incorrect because coming in before school might be helpful but only if it is arranged in advance with her teachers. Answer D is incorrect because giving her a deadline may overwhelm her and make it difficult for her to complete any of her work.

65. A: Neuroimaging studies find that the left side of the (A) parietal lobe, located behind the frontal lobe at the back of the top of the brain, is most involved with mathematical calculations. The frontal (B) lobe is involved with speech, emotions, and executive functions such as solving problems, making decisions, and planning. The occipital (C) lobe is at the back of the brain and is responsible for the processing of information received through the sense of vision. The temporal (D) lobe is below the frontal and parietal lobes and is involved with aspects of speech, memory, perceiving and identifying auditory stimuli (sounds), and other functions. Damage in the parietal-temporal area can cause deficits in digit span and verbal memory.

66. C: Curriculum-based assessments can be valuable tools in monitoring a student's progress compared with what his or her IEP goals are. These are typically quick assessments that give the teacher data right away. Answer A is incorrect because curriculum-based assessments typically compare students to their own growth rather than determine grade level. Answer B is incorrect because curriculum-based assessments are separate from classroom grades. Answer D is incorrect because it would likely not end up in a student's school file.

67. A: One of the disadvantages to teaching students individually is that they cannot interact with their peers. It can be beneficial for students to work with their peers in order to build social skills and learn from each other. Although there are many advantages to one-on-one groups, many students learn best with other students. Answer B is incorrect because group size does not affect whether a pull-out group focuses on general education curriculum. Answer C is incorrect because students also don't have access to general education teachers in any kind of special education pull-out group. Answer D is incorrect because students have access to the special education curriculum with either pull-out group type.

68. B: Although there are many pros and cons to co-teaching, one of the advantages is that both teachers are familiar with the content and can plan together. When special education teachers are supporting the general education classroom teachers, they do not have this opportunity. This can cause special education teachers to have difficulty while supporting students in content they are not familiar with or experts in. Answer A is incorrect because special education teachers will likely still have the same amount of time to plan either way. Answer C is incorrect because special education teachers have the opportunity to differentiate instruction in either one of these models. Answer D is incorrect because collaborating with classroom teachers should be used in every method when assisting students with disabilities.

69. B: Multisensory strategies, including the use of touch in manipulating letters or tapping the letters with their fingers, can be effective strategies for students with dyslexia. This sensory approach allows them to break down words and memorize them in different ways. Answer A is incorrect because the whole-word approach does not tend to be as effective for students with dyslexia. Answers C is incorrect because, while it may be useful, modeling is not as effective for addressing reading skills as using multisensory strategies. Answer D is incorrect because graphic organizers typically help students with comprehension and idea organization rather than with the reading challenges typically associated with dyslexia.

70. C: Using a survey to identify students' favorite reinforcers (C) is not an example of a strategy to improve generalization skills. It is an example of a strategy to improve students' motivation. Assigning field trips, role plays (A), simulations, etc., for students to apply their new learning is a good way to encourage them to use what they have learned in class to other situations; the teacher should give students feedback on their applications. Real-life situations are also excellent for generalizing learned skills. Multiple-choice games involving analogies (B) help students apply learning by showing their understanding of relationships among concepts or objects. Having students exercise their math skills in activities like loan financing, balancing accounts, and using money (D) is a good way to help them not only apply what they know to real life, but also to realize some of the realistic, practical purposes and uses of their learning.

71. B: Obsessive Compulsive Disorder (OCD). Children and adults with OCD typically engage in a series of highly ritualized behaviors that are rigidly performed when they feel stressed. Behaviors include tapping, snapping fingers, blinking, counting and so forth.

72. B: Meet with the specialist to discuss the teacher's goals. It isn't possible to determine if strategies are effective or determine a future course unless the teacher has a firm grasp of his goals and expectations.

73. C: Although all of these choices may be examples of some kind of formative assessment, observing her in class is most likely to provide the best data. Formative assessments are designed to assess what the student knows as the learning occurs. In order to monitor progress using formative assessments, it is important to take a look at the areas the student struggles in and if she is improving. Answer A is incorrect because interviewing a first grader like Andrea may not always provide the most accurate data. Answer B is incorrect because giving her academic probes would not show how she is developing on her overall social and behavioral skills as well as observation would. Answer D is incorrect because simply monitoring how she does on tests may not provide the whole picture in how she is developing overall.

74. C: Although all these choices can help in making sure the classroom is a safe environment, reporting student behavior to the parents immediately can be most effective. When students misbehave, this must be communicated to the parents so further action can potentially be taken. If it is not reported to parents, students may continue with these poor behaviors and put other students at risk. Answer A is incorrect because simply sending home the class rules may not work for every parent, and they may not always keep track of them. Answer B is incorrect because although getting to know the background of the parents might be helpful, this may not benefit the safety of the class. Answer D is incorrect because only reporting the positive behavior can help to build a safe classroom, but it is more important to report negative behavior that might be a safety concern.

75. B: Although it is possible that the occupational therapist would provide services to a student with a hearing impairment, this is not typically the case. Occupational therapists often provide support to students who struggle with motor skills in the school setting. Students with hearing impairments may or may not have these needs, and it is important to understand the areas in which students have needs in order to consult with the appropriate service providers. Answer A is incorrect because speech-language pathologists typically assist students with hearing impairments in working on communication skills. Answer C is incorrect because the school nurse is an important member of the team in determining the health care services that the student may need at school. Answer D is incorrect because the audiologist typically conducts the hearing screening to determine the impact of the hearing impairment.

76. C: The Wechsler Adult Intelligence Scale (WAIS) is an intelligence test, but it is not designed for students who do not use verbal communication. The Merrill-Palmer Scale is for assessing intellectual functioning in children from 18 months to four years old. Raven's Progressive Matrices have three levels: one that is colored for students who have mental or physical disabilities, one that is standard for students aged 6-16 and 17+ years, and one that is advanced for students aged 12-16 and 17+ years. The Leiter International Performance Scale-Revised is for children aged 2 to 18 years.

77. A: A number of researchers have found that assisted reading methods achieve significant improvements in students' reading fluency. Methods using repeated readings can be both unassisted and assisted (B). Assisted reading methods, because of the need for one-on-one instruction, have been found more workable in tutoring, but they are too time-intensive to be incorporated successfully in traditional classrooms (C). Reading while listening takes less time by being adapted using recordings for instruction of a group rather than individual students. It is thus more efficient than assisted reading, but it is not unrelated (D) because it was adapted from assisted reading.

78. A: When parents request an IEE, the testing must be administered by someone who is not employed by the school district. Parents have the right to request an IEE when they do not agree with the results of a special education evaluation. The school must consider the results of this evaluation in order to ensure that it is providing FAPE. Answer B is incorrect because although the IEP team must consider the results of the evaluation, they do not have to accept them. Answer C is incorrect because parents are not automatically required to pay for the IEE. When parents request an IEE, the district must either provide the IEE at public expense or request a due process hearing to defend its evaluation. Answer D is incorrect because an explanation is not required for the parents to request an IEE.

79. C: One of the characteristics of an effective lesson plan is positive feedback. Reinforcing student behavior is one of the most effective ways to praise students and provide this positive feedback. Answer A is incorrect because selectively calling on students may create an imbalance of who gets called on. Answer B is incorrect because it is best to give students some time to think after asking a question. Answer D is incorrect because feedback should be provided immediately so they can make corrections.

80. D: Students with attention-deficit/hyperactivity disorder are generally extremely sensitive to distractions. A learning environment in which visual and audio distractions have been eliminated is best. Low lighting, few posters, and a clean whiteboard will help minimize distractions.

Practice Test #3

1. Which of the following instructional strategies would be most appropriate when teaching a science lesson to a third-grade class?

a. Reciprocal teaching
b. Socratic questioning
c. Direct instruction
d. Learning centers

2. Why might it be difficult to incorporate different kinds of activities each day when teaching a class with students of varying disabilities?

a. Some students require structure in their daily routine.
b. Some students may not have the knowledge required for each activity.
c. Some students may not be comfortable working with other students.
d. Some students require specific activities in their IEPs.

3. When interpreting the results of a norm-referenced test, how are the scores determined?

a. By comparing a student's score to a previous score
b. By comparing a student's score to other students that are the same age
c. By comparing a student's score to a standard deviation
d. By comparing a student's score to other students with disabilities

4. Which of the following accommodations would be the LEAST useful for visually impaired students?

a. Screen magnification
b. Text reader application
c. Screen reader software
d. Simplified versions of texts and class content

5. Which of the following best describes when a formative assessment would take place in the classroom?

a. Before the instruction
b. While the students are learning
c. After the learning has been completed
d. At any time during a lesson

6. When planning a lesson for a group of students with severe needs working on life skills, which of the following types of practice would most likely be used to ensure that they understand the material?

a. Guided practice
b. Collaborative practice
c. Independent practice
d. Student-led practice

7. Which of the following is *most* accurate about exceptional students who are gifted?

a. They typically have advanced social skills.
b. Their academic performance is superior.
c. Their IQ scores indicate their giftedness.
d. They typically have difficulty relating to peers.

8. Which of the following is true about reading?

a. Students can best learn to read through reading to learn
b. Students can learn to read and read to learn concurrently
c. Students cannot read to learn until after learning to read
d. Students in early grades will not read unless it is to learn content

9. Rachel is a student with a traumatic brain injury in a life skills class working on job interviewing skills. Which of the following would be the most appropriate summative assessment for this unit?

a. Assigning a paper
b. Assigning a multiple-choice test
c. Assigning a presentation
d. Assigning a mock interview

10. Which of the following is NOT a good example of adapting education to maximize the physical abilities of students with specialized needs?

a. Wyatt, who cannot write with a pen but can use his fists, answers test questions using a computer with a touch screen.
b. Fabian, who is blind and does not read Braille, listens to recorded test questions on a tape player with earphones, answering by pressing buttons on a counter.
c. Sue, who has impaired vision and impaired fine motor skills, takes a pen and paper test along with the rest of the students in her class.
d. Donnie, who is deaf, can participate in school fire drills because the school has both sound alarms and strobe lights.

11. Which of the following would be the best example of using technology to meet the needs of all kinds of learners?

a. Giving a slide show presentation
b. Grouping students to use tablets
c. Providing audiobooks to each student
d. Allowing students to use computers for independent research

12. Joaquin's family has recently immigrated to the USA from another country. He speaks only a little English. According to US federal law, which of the following is true?

a. Joaquin cannot be determined to be disabled solely due to limited English proficiency.
b. Joaquin must only attend regular classes despite his language.
c. Joaquin should be labeled as disabled to get him into ESL classes.
d. Joaquin should go to a school emphasizing his first language.

13. Which of the following types of groups would be most beneficial for a low-achieving student?

a. Homogeneous group
b. Heterogeneous group
c. Achievement group
d. Learning group

14. Justin is a ninth-grade student with a specific learning disability in the area of reading comprehension. Which of the following strategies would be most effective in ensuring that he maintains his knowledge of a story?

a. Asking him to read the story three times in a row
b. Asking him to reread the story for homework
c. Asking him to reread the story each week
d. Asking him to quiz himself on the story

15. Kevin is an eighth grader with behavioral challenges, which makes it difficult for him to stay in the classroom. What would be the best strategy to ensure that he is able to access the general education curriculum?

a. Allowing him to complete less work than the other students
b. Having him complete his work outside of the classroom
c. Requiring that he complete only the work he does in the classroom
d. Allowing him to stay in the classroom without completing work and just listening to instruction

16. Which of the following is an example of a personal cultural bias that may impact communication with a student or their family?

a. Hesitating to contact a student's family because of a past encounter with the family
b. Hesitating to contact a student's family because of an unfamiliarity with their history
c. Hesitating to contact a student's family because of an experience with a sibling
d. Hesitating to contact a student's family because of the community that they live in

17. Which statement is most likely to be true?

a. All teachers should do whatever is necessary to acquire basic knowledge of common symptoms of special needs in children, as well as typical interventions and strategies for instructing high-needs students.
b. Teachers are always the most equipped individuals to determine a child's individual needs and interventions; however, most schools require evaluation by a professional.
c. All children should be considered "high-needs;" teachers should teach each child as though he or she may have learning difficulties when instructing and guiding them.
d. Students with learning or physiological challenges are best served in separate classrooms, where they can get the specialized attention and services they deserve.

18. A special education teacher assigns his students a collaborative group project. Which strategy would be most effective to benefit all students in the group?

a. Assigning one student the task of compiling and presenting the group's work
b. Allowing students to volunteer to make contributions to the project
c. Leading the activities himself and directing what the students do
d. Assigning each student an equal number of duties related to the project

19. A classroom includes one student with visual impairment, two students with hearing impairments, three students with Down syndrome, and four with other intellectual disabilities. In addition to special education teachers, which of the following other professionals are most likely to be included in delivering special education services (excluding testing) to this group?

a. Physical therapist, occupational therapist, behavior specialist
b. Physical therapist, speech-language pathologist, orientation & mobility specialist, behavior specialist
c. Orientation and mobility specialist, physical therapist, school psychologist, audiologist
d. Audiologist, speech-language pathologist, orientation & mobility specialist, occupational therapist

20. Cathy has coexisting conditions of spina bifida and related health problems, intellectual disabilities, deafness, and autism. She engages in self-injurious behavior in response to physical distress. Which of the following is most likely true?

a. The self-injurious behavior is an aberration that serves no purpose.
b. The self-injurious behavior is an attempt to communicate a need.
c. The self-injurious behavior is caused by her intellectual disabilities.
d. The self-injurious behavior is caused by her autism diagnosis.

21. A student displays a slight learning disability, which mostly effects reading and writing development. He is removed from the general student body to receive special education. While this student's disability has put him behind in his English class, he is not behind in any other class. What has the school violated in removing this student from the general student body?

a. Individual Education Plan
b. Human Rights Act
c. Americans with Disabilities Act
d. Least Restrictive Environment (LRE)

22. Among all persons with learning disabilities, what proportion has reading disorders?

a. 20%
b. 40%
c. 60%
d. 80%

23. Which of the following is not true about the universal design approach to instruction?

a. It benefits LD students only with the required adaptations
b. It provides various methods of presenting subject content
c. It affords flexibility among different instructional strategies
d. It allows different ways of demonstrating content mastery

24. What can a teacher do in regard to the physical environment of the classroom to increase attention and learning?

a. Cover every wall with posters
b. Play music
c. Ensure the class is brightly lit
d. Arrange the desks in a circle

25. Which would be the best interpretation of a student who performs well on tests and standardized assessments but generally has low scores for smaller assessments such as classwork and homework?

a. The tests and standardized assessments are poorly constructed.
b. The student does not give his or her best effort on classwork and homework.
c. The standardized tests are not age appropriate for the student.
d. The standardized tests are a better indicator than the other assessments.

26. Typical cognitive development in a child between the ages of 2 and 6 would consist of which of the following?

a. A child that manipulates objects
b. A child that uses perception in their thought process
c. A child that applies logical reasoning
d. A child that has abstract thoughts

27. Jenny is a student teacher majoring in special education. She is working with a small group of students who are six years old and have mild developmental delays. She wants to give them some Piagetian tasks to try. Which of these would be most appropriate?

a. Tasks involving conservation of numbers, using rows of the same number of pennies, pebbles, or beads, arranged different distances apart
b. Class inclusion tasks using pictures and a 20-questions game to figure out which one the teacher is thinking of
c. Tasks involving conservation of weight, using boxes filled with sand arranged differently (e.g., stacked or side by side)
d. Tasks involving conservation of volume, using liquid in differently shaped containers (e.g., a tall, skinny container and a short, wide container)

28. If you are making a functional skills assessment for a secondary school student with an intellectual disability, which of following should you obtain?

a. A vocational skills assessment
b. Up-to-date IQ testing results
c. Tests of motor development
d. Scholastic Aptitude Test score

29. Jessica is a six-year-old kindergarten student. Which description may indicate typical language development?

a. She speaks in sentences of five to six words.
b. She has a vocabulary of 500 words.
c. She holds up her fingers to tell her age.
d. She uses phrases such as "me want"

30. In order for students to make progress on their IEP goals, which of the following makes the most sense when grouping students for a math intervention group?

a. Grouping students based on their ability level
b. Grouping students based on their grade level
c. Grouping students based on their teachers
d. Grouping students based on their maturity level

31. Which of the following would be the most effective long-term strategy in maintaining a safe classroom environment?

a. Showing the students where the exits are
b. Ensuring that the classroom is clean and orderly
c. Posting the class rules on the wall
d. Establishing positive relationships with the students

32. Which of the following is an example of a fine motor skill that a four-year-old student would be expected to do?

a. Hop on one foot
b. Catch a ball
c. Cut with scissors
d. Ride a tricycle

33. Which of the following students would it be most appropriate to conduct a verbal intelligence test on when reevaluating for special education services?

a. A student with an intellectual disability
b. A student with a specific learning disability in math
c. A student with a specific learning disability in writing
d. A student with a visual impairment

34. An ORF is an:

a. Oral Reading Fluency assessment
b. Occasional Reading Function assessment
c. Oscar Reynolds Feinstein assessment
d. Oral Reading Failure assessment

35. What is the primary strategy for supporting students who prefer structured routines over dynamic schedules and who are upset by sudden changes?

a. Maintaining the same schedule as much as possible
b. Giving advance warning of changes, such as a visitor or school assembly
c. Allowing students who are likely to be upset to stay next to the teacher or a friend who can comfort them
d. Teaching relaxation techniques

36. When lesson planning for a life skills class for students with severe needs, which element is often considered the most important to include?

a. Objectives
b. Warmup
c. Direct instruction
d. Practical application

37. Which one of the following disability categories is likely to have the greatest impact on individuals across their life span?

a. Developmental delays
b. Speech or language impairments
c. Multiple disabilities
d. Specific learning disabilities

38. When conducting an assessment in the area of fine motor skills, which of the following activities would be the most important to observe?

a. Watching a student draw a picture
b. Watching a student make numbers with their hands
c. Watching a student throw a ball
d. Watching a student ride a bike

39. A calculator would be best categorized as which type of assistive technology?

a. Low tech
b. Mid tech
c. High tech
d. No tech

40. When working with students on writing their names in a kindergarten class, which of the following would be the LEAST effective in generalizing this skill?

a. Asking students to practice in the classroom during free time
b. Asking students to practice at home with their parents
c. Asking students to practice when they go to art class
d. Asking students to practice with their friends

41. Which of the following is the best reason to implement cooperative learning into classrooms with students with disabilities?

a. Students are more likely to engage in this structure.
b. Students receive more support in these kinds of classrooms.
c. Students receive more instruction from teachers with this model.
d. Students are more likely to meet IEP goals in this environment.

42. Of the following instructional strategies used, which is most likely to support LD students in taking risks during reading lessons in a large group/class setting?

a. Assigning students to pairs to discuss teacher questions about the lesson
b. Asking students to give summaries reviewing the main points of a lesson
c. Having students complete reminder worksheets at the end of the lesson
d. Inviting students to ask "who," "what," or "where" questions on a lesson

43. Zachary is a 10th-grade student who receives special education services as a student with another health impairment due to his ADHD, and he struggles to sit still for long periods of time. Which of the following strategies would be most effective in providing opportunities for Zachary to move around?

a. Giving Zachary a pass to move around when he needs to
b. Giving Zachary a timer to get up and stretch every 10 minutes
c. Organizing the classroom so that Zachary has his own area
d. Incorporating movement activities for the entire class

44. Which of the following occurs when someone gives in to peer pressure and does something he or she would normally not do in order to be accepted into a group?

a. Conformity
b. Independence
c. Guilt
d. Individualism

45. When teaching an eighth-grade geography class with multiple students who require additional support personnel in the class, which is the best strategy for organizing the classroom?

a. Having rows of desks
b. Having desk clusters
c. Having desks in circles
d. Having long tables

46. Marissa is an 11th-grade student who accesses special education services as a student with autism spectrum disorder. Which of the following lesson plan elements would likely be most beneficial in meeting her needs in her math class?

a. Providing a cross-curricular curriculum
b. Providing multiple tasks to complete
c. Providing multiple choices
d. Providing hands-on instruction

47. Which of the following occurs between the ages of 3 years and 5 years?

a. Children demonstrate mastery of complex grammar.
b. Children begin to use sarcasm and argue their points of view in detail.
c. Children experience a considerable increase in vocabulary
d. Children become able to retell fictional narratives with complete plots, resolutions, and character motivations.

48. At the beginning of the week, a special education teacher asked a group of students to generate a list of verbs that make visual or sound pictures. She suggests students think of verbs for walking, talking, eating, sitting, and playing. The students spend the remainder of the week compiling the list. They notice interesting verbs as they read books, remark on less common verbs they hear in conversation or on television, and locate interesting verbs in signs, magazines, and other printed materials. One child begins to draw pictures to illustrate some of the verbs. Two children collaborate to create a play in which they demonstrate some of the verbs in a dance. A boy writes a song incorporating the list of verbs. The project is extremely successful. At the end of the week, the students have created the following list:

> TIPTOE, SCOOT, MUMBLE, MUNCH, LEAP, SPIN, DIVE, POUNCE, GLIDE, SLITHER, MOAN, WHISPER, GRUMBLE, NIBBLE, SHRILL, HOLLER, PERCH, LEAN, STOMP, MARCH, GIGGLE, HOP, STRUT, SLOUCH, GULP, HOWL, WHINE, SLURP, CROUCH, DRIBBLE, DROOL, HOOT, YELP, YOWL, GROWL, WHISTLE, SHRIEK, SNICKER, INSULT, COMPLIMENT, PLEAD, BARK, WIGGLE, TWIST, SLINK, TODDLE, TRUDGE, WANDER, STROLL.

The teacher's goal is to:

a. Enhance students' understanding of theme by encouraging them to make connections between categories of verbs.
b. Enhance students' vocabulary by encouraging them to find examples in the world around them.
c. Enhance students' understanding of context by encouraging them to explore verbs for contextual clues.
d. Enhance students' sense of curiosity by directing their attention to a number of different resources they may not have considered.

49. Ricky is a seventh-grade student being evaluated for special education services who is administered an IQ test. Which of the following best describes the results of his test if he scored a 100?

a. Ricky scored in the average range.
b. Ricky got all the questions correct.
c. Ricky does not need special education services.
d. Ricky does need special education services.

50. Which of the following best describes how technology can be included in a small group of students with disabilities working on reading comprehension?

a. Accessing audiobooks to listen to the story
b. Using computers to research the author of the story
c. Accessing speech-to-text software to answer questions
d. Using tablets to read a story and answer questions

51. Which of the following best describes how the results of an intelligence test can guide instruction?

a. To determine whether a student qualifies for special education services
b. To determine whether a student has an emotional disability
c. To determine which accommodations students should access
d. To determine whether a student has a learning disability

52. When writing learning objectives for a lesson plan, the S in SMART stands for Specific: an objective should specify what students will achieve and in what amount. Which of the following correctly identifies one of the other initials in the SMART acronym?

a. M stands for Memorable
b. A stands for Activities
c. R stands for Resources
d. T stands for Time-based

53. Which of the following strategies is likely to be most effective in overcoming any kind of personal cultural biases when working with students with disabilities?

a. Learning about why the cultural bias occurs
b. Being objective when evaluating these students
c. Treating each of the students the same way
d. Encouraging cross-group participation among peers

54. Jessica is a ninth-grade student who struggles with becoming distracted while she works in the general education setting. Which of the following methods of differentiated instruction would be most beneficial to Jessica?

a. Differentiating the learning environment
b. Differentiating the content
c. Differentiating the process
d. Differentiating the product

55. Which of the following is the best strategy for teaching students with coexisting disabilities?

a. Teaching to each disability separately
b. Teaching to the student as a whole
c. Teaching to the needs of the most impacted disability
d. Teaching to both disabilities at the same time

56. Suzie is a sixth-grade student with a specific learning disability whose parents have little or no involvement and typically do not respond when the school contacts them. Which of the following strategies would be most effective in involving them in the IEP process?

a. Continuing to reach out to them until they respond
b. Sending home forms for them to fill out
c. Offering that they participate in the meeting by phone
d. Trying to get a hold of a grandparent or relative

57. Corey is a second-grade student who receives special education services due to a specific learning disability in the area of reading fluency. Which of the following is the best strategy for ensuring success for Corey if he is severely impacted by his reading fluency deficiencies?

a. Providing additional support in the classroom
b. Pulling Corey for small-group reading fluency intervention
c. Modifying the material that Corey is to complete
d. Pulling Corey for one-to-one reading fluency intervention

58. James has severe cerebral palsy and is nonverbal and nonambulatory. He cannot read or write, but he has excellent receptive language skills and can answer yes/no questions. Due to severe contractures, he cannot use his fingers or hands functionally, but he can grasp an object inserted into his fist. You are ordering adaptive equipment for him. Which would be the best choice?

a. A communication board with a pointer
b. A computer with a keyboard
c. A voice-activated computer
d. An adaptive holder enabling him to manipulate a pen

59. In the first week of school, a resource teacher asks her high school students to make lists of things they know how to do well. How is this activity most useful to the teacher?

a. It establishes a feeling of success in her students from the start.
b. It is an informal assessment of their writing skills and gives the teacher an idea of each student's interests and abilities.
c. It is a formal assessment of prior knowledge.
d. It invites further discussion of each student's unique contributions and will help the class bond with mutual respect.

60. Which end-of-unit assessment would BEST allow students to demonstrate their executive functioning skills?

a. End-of-unit test
b. End-of-unit essay
c. End-of-unit presentation
d. End-of-unit performance task

61. Which of the following is most accurate regarding textbooks that elementary school teachers use when teaching culturally diverse students?

a. Textbooks introduce many new concepts in a short time for such students.
b. Teacher editions commonly offer tips for meeting diverse students' needs.
c. The reading levels of most textbooks are appropriate for diverse students.
d. Most textbooks eliminate the need for much differentiation of instruction.

62. Which of the following classroom organization methods would be most beneficial for a teacher who includes a lot of classroom discussions?

a. Including a meeting area in the classroom
b. Arranging the desks facing toward each other
c. Having tables instead of desks
d. Ensuring that each student can move around

63. Which of the following is true about learned helplessness and students with disabilities?

a. Students with disabilities typically do not suffer from learned helplessness.
b. Students with disabilities often learn to control situations.
c. Students with disabilities tend to reach out for help before they get to learned helplessness.
d. Students with disabilities often feel like they have no control.

64. A student is taking a reading test. The teacher has blocked out a number of words. Each blank is assigned a set of three possible words. The student must select the correct word from each set so that the text makes sense. The student is taking:

a. A cloze test
b. A maze test
c. A multiple-choice quiz
d. A vocabulary test

65. Parker is a sixth-grade student who receives special education services as a student with a specific learning disability. Which of the following responsibilities would the special education teacher always need to perform while assisting a student like Parker?

a. Monitoring the progress of his IEP goals
b. Providing mental health support
c. Ensuring he has access to modifications
d. Providing executive functioning interventions

66. Javier is a fourth-grade student with an emotional disturbance. Which one of the following individuals is LEAST likely to attend IEP meetings?

a. School psychologist
b. Director of special education
c. The student
d. School principal

67. Standardized tests can be a valuable assessment tool in evaluating students who receive special education services. When would state-mandated standardized tests be inappropriate to use for data in measuring student growth or progress?

a. When evaluating students who take alternate assessments
b. When evaluating students new to the school
c. When evaluating students who have frequent absences
d. When evaluating students with accommodations

68. What would be the best warm-up for a lesson on adding and subtracting fractions?

a. Multiplying and dividing fractions
b. Adding and subtracting fractions
c. Multiplying and dividing whole numbers
d. Adding and subtracting whole numbers

69. Shirley's objective is to get 90% of math problems correct on each test for eight consecutive weekly tests. On the graph below, the highest point is 90%. Based on this information, when evaluating the effectiveness of the instructional program made for Shirley, which is the most valid conclusion?

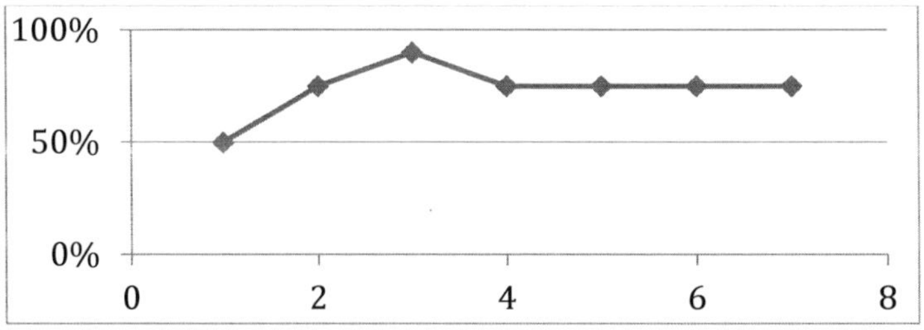

a. Shirley's program needs re-evaluation because, being stuck at 75%, she may be unable to reach 90%.
b. Shirley's program needs re-evaluation to become more challenging as she is consistently successful.
c. Shirley's program needs re-evaluation because she has reached a plateau below objective criterion.
d. Shirley's program needs no change as she has improved, is consistent, and simply needs more time.

70. Which of the following grouping techniques would likely be least effective when working with a small reading intervention group at an elementary school?

a. Grouping by ability
b. Grouping by age
c. Grouping by disability
d. Grouping by behavior

71. Bert and Nan are first graders receiving special education. They each have an IEP objective in reading/phonological awareness to produce rhyming words and distinguish rhyming from non-rhyming words. Bert is blind, and Nan has cerebral palsy with poor fine motor skills. Which of the following would be the best plan for both students to work on this objective?

a. Give both a worksheet with a list of word pairs and have each student circle the pairs that rhyme and cross through the pairs that do not rhyme.
b. Read a list of word pairs to both students and have each raise the left hand if the words do not rhyme and the right hand if they do rhyme.
c. Give Nan a worksheet with a list of word pairs, having her circle the rhyming pairs and cross out the non-rhyming pairs; read word pairs to Bert and have him raise his right or left hand to indicate if they rhyme or not.
d. Give Nan a list of word pairs, have her read them to Bert, and have him indicate by which hand he raises whether they rhyme or not.

72. Mr. Law wants to facilitate his high school students' ability to expand their vocabulary. He seizes the opportunity when a student comes in perplexed at having seen the word "antidisestablishmentarianism." He asks the class, "What parts of this word have you seen before in other words?" One student volunteers that he recognizes "anti-" from "antibiotic;" another says "Anti-Trust Law." A third student then identifies "dis-" from "disability" and a fourth says "dislike." Most of the class then sees the next parts as "establish" or "establishment." He then asks them if they have seen other words ending in "-ary" and, following their responses, "-ism." What technique is Mr. Law using?

a. Multiple exposures to a word
b. Choosing appropriate words
c. Making a contextual analysis
d. Teaching them word analysis

73. What is correct regarding making environmental changes and administering reinforcements for managing the behavior of students with emotional or behavioral disturbances?

a. The measures taken should be uniform across all students and types of behaviors.
b. The measures taken should vary in accordance with the intensity of the behaviors.
c. The measures taken should always begin with more intrusion and gradually decrease.
d. The measures taken should always begin with more intensity, fading with progress.

74. Samuel is a student with a specific learning disability in the area of oral expression. What kind of assessment would be most appropriate in order to evaluate his continued eligibility?

a. Expressive language
b. Receptive language
c. Auditory discrimination
d. Verbal intelligence

75. Which one of the following environmental factors is likely to have the greatest impact on students who receive special education services due to mental health concerns?

a. Sleep deprivation
b. Smoking
c. Exposure to toxins
d. Substance abuse

76. Which of the following is true regarding alternate curriculum programs?

a. These programs are the first choice for students identified with disabilities
b. A student's eligibility for these programs is determined by his/her IEP team
c. They are preferable to general curricula with accommodations/modifications
d. Students are primarily assigned to general education classrooms in these programs

77. What would be the MOST beneficial in supplementing the daily math curriculum of a 10th-grade student with Down syndrome who is working on functional skills?

a. Including addition fact worksheets
b. Including time-telling worksheets
c. Including measuring worksheets
d. Including order-of-operations worksheets

78. Which of these pairs of tests is most amenable to comparison of aptitude with performance?

a. WISC and WRAT
b. WIAT and WRAT
c. WISC and WIAT
d. None of these

79. Alex is a ninth-grade student who receives services as a student with a traumatic brain injury. In order to be eligible to receive services under this disability category, which of the following causes of the injury can be ruled out?

a. Birth trauma
b. Combat injuries
c. Violence
d. Sports-related injuries

80. Which of the following best supports differentiated instruction?

a. Lecturing in a clear voice and using simple language
b. Assigning the same essay to all students
c. Offering a choice of an essay, presentation, or video for the final project
d. Bringing in guest speakers of various nationalities

Answer Key and Explanations for Test #3

1. D: When teaching a science lesson to a group of third-grade students, it is important to incorporate hands-on learning activities. Learning centers can provide opportunities for these students to do activities and learn about different topics. Learning centers are most appropriate for younger students, such as a group of third graders. Answer A is incorrect because reciprocal teaching would be most appropriate for older students who are capable of teaching each other rather than younger students. Answer B is incorrect because Socratic questioning would be most appropriate for higher level questioning based on thoughtful dialogue between the teacher and student and is a skill that third graders likely would not have. Answer C is incorrect because direct instruction may be more appropriate for a more abstract topic such as reading or math, as it does not promote hands-on exploration and investigation.

2. A: Although it is typically thought of as a good teaching practice to incorporate different kinds of activities in a lesson, some students struggle with this change. Students with autism or ADHD may have a harder time adjusting to their daily routine being adjusted. Incorporating some elements of the same activity every day might be best for some students' needs. Answer B is incorrect because even if students do not all have the knowledge that is required, the activity might be designed to give them that knowledge. Answer C is incorrect because it is best practice to monitor which students can work together and which students cannot. Answer D is incorrect because though it is important to implement the activities a student can complete according to their IEP, a variety of activities should still be offered so that each student can still feel included in the class.

3. B: Norm-referenced tests can be helpful in comparing a student's score with a random sample of other students that are of the same age. This allows the evaluator to determine areas of strength and weakness for students by comparing them to others. It is important to understand where the average score stands when interpreting assessment results in order to determine appropriate instruction or programming. Answer A is incorrect because comparing a student's score to a previous score would be considered progress monitoring. Answer C is incorrect because it is important to consider where the standard deviation is when interpreting results, but the score cannot be compared to a standard deviation. Answer D is incorrect because these assessments compare all of the students, not just those with disabilities.

4. C: Screen magnification, text reader applications, and screen reader software can all be useful for visually impaired students, though fully blind students will not experience benefits from screen magnification. Unless they have a separate disability or impairment, the complexity of texts and content is not the issue for visually impaired students. Simplifying texts and class content for these students would not help them access class content.

5. B: Formative assessments are designed to measure student progress while the students are learning in order to gauge what they can do. These tend to be more informal assessments that are not associated with a grade. Formative assessments can be beneficial for students with disabilities in guiding what level of support they may need as instruction moves on. Answer a is incorrect because the assessment before the instruction would typically be the diagnostic. Answer c is incorrect because the summative assessment typically occurs after the learning has been completed. Answer d is incorrect because it is most beneficial for students to give them a formative assessment during their learning in order to guide instruction.

6. A: In order for students to learn from the lecture, it is important that they are able to practice it on their own. Students with significant needs may have a difficult time going straight from a lecture to independent practice, so guided practice is crucial. This gives them an opportunity to understand how to complete the practice. Answer B is incorrect because collaborative practice may not be as beneficial for students who need support from the teacher. Answer C is incorrect because independent practice for students with severe needs is a difficult task. Answer D is incorrect because student-led practice may not provide the results wanted without supervision from a teacher.

7. D: Some gifted students excel in all areas, including athletics and social skills (A), but not necessarily. Gifted children can have different abilities and interests than peers, making social interaction awkward. They may have difficulty relating to peers with more typical abilities and interests, resulting in peers who may not want to interact with them for being different. Some gifted children prefer academic/creative activities over social activities. Some gifted children show superior academic performance (B), while some do not. Some are bored by traditional curricula (including special education for the gifted) and lack motivation, while some use unconventional methods. As a child, Albert Einstein reportedly was failed in math by a teacher for achieving correct answers without following prescribed steps. Not all gifted children get high IQ scores (C) because giftedness also includes creativity or other forms not represented by IQ scores, not just intelligence. Some gifted children do not respond to standardized measures because they may think differently and/or be uninterested in test items.

8. C: Students typically learn to read through third grade and transition to reading to learn and reading for pleasure around fourth grade. While they are learning the basics, much of their attention is focused on decoding, word recognition, vocabulary, and comprehension. While students may begin to gain content knowledge from text, their primary focus is on learning to read, so reading to learn is not the main goal at this stage. Later, in upper elementary grades, independent reading to learn complex content becomes the dominant purpose. This explains why (B) is the best option.

9. D: Assigning a mock interview is the most appropriate demonstration of knowledge when working on interviewing for a job. Summative assessments evaluate what a student learns from a particular unit, and a mock interview is the best way to demonstrate this knowledge. It is important for the summative assessment to show whether or not the student has the skills needed or the knowledge that was supposed to be gained in that unit. Answer a is incorrect because assigning a paper would not likely be very beneficial to students who are practicing for job interviews. Answer b is incorrect because a multiple-choice test would not help students as much as practicing the skills that they will need. Answer c is incorrect because although a presentation may be helpful, a mock interview would be more productive in seeing what a student is capable of by the end of the unit.

10. C: Wyatt cannot write but can use his fists, so a computer touch screen is a good way for him to record his test answers. This is a good example of adapting lessons; therefore, option A is incorrect.

Fabian cannot take a test visually, so his teacher has provided recorded questions, and he presses buttons to record his answers. This is a good example of adapting lessons; therefore, option B is incorrect.

Sue cannot see as well as other students in her class and cannot use a pen as well as others, yet she is taking a pen and paper test despite her visual and manual disabilities. This is not a good example of adapting lessons; therefore, option C is correct.

Donnie cannot hear the sound of a fire alarm, but the school has added strobe lights, which he can see, so he can participate in fire drills. This is a good example of adaptive education; therefore, option D is incorrect.

11. B: In order to use technology to meet the needs of all kinds of learners, it is important to allow students some freedom to learn using the method that meets their needs. When students are able to access their peers, they can learn using a variety of methods including collaboration. This allows the students to work with each other in a variety of ways while using the tablet, which may include videos, articles, and other types of projects. Answer A is incorrect because a slide show presentation likely will only target a certain group of students in the class. Answer C is incorrect because audiobooks may be beneficial to some students but not to others. Answer D is incorrect because simply giving them computers may not be productive for each student in the class to work independently.

12. A: By US federal law, Joaquin cannot be determined to be disabled solely because of his limited English proficiency (A). IDEA 2004 states that in addition to lack of instruction in reading or math, a student "....must not be determined to be a child with a disability...if the determinant factor...is...limited English proficiency." It is not true that Joaquin must only attend regular classes (B); there are classes and teachers for ESL (English as a Second Language) and ELL (English Language Learners) students in America. Depending on students' levels of comprehension and expression in English and the individual school's resources, they may receive ESL instruction part of the day and attend regular classrooms part of the day, or they may have all of their instruction from ESL or ELL teachers until they achieve greater English proficiency. Joaquin should not be classified as disabled to get him into ESL classes (C). This is illegal as well as unnecessary. A student cannot and need not be determined disabled for this purpose. There is no federal law mandating that a student like Joaquin must go to a school that emphasizes his first language (D).

13. B: When done properly, grouping students can be beneficial. Teachers can create a heterogeneous group, mixing high and low achievers in the same work group, which will allow low achievers to learn from high achievers. Grouping all low achievers in one group typically does not result in a significant increase in academic performance. Conversely, grouping all high achievers together has been shown to result in increases in academic performance. Teachers should carefully assess the abilities of their students prior to creating groups. Additionally, teachers should regularly assess work groups to ensure that students are meeting expectations and to address issues or concerns that arise after the groups are created.

14. C: When maintaining a skill, it is important to practice that skill periodically over the course of time. For someone that struggles with reading comprehension, it is important to practice reading multiple times to ensure that the content is remembered. Students with disabilities who struggle in certain areas will likely need extra practice for maintaining these skills. Answer A is incorrect because simply reading the story a few times in a row will not allow the student to maintain the skill long-term. Answer B is incorrect because just rereading the story once for homework likely will not allow him to maintain the skill either. Answer D is incorrect because although quizzing himself may be a valuable strategy in helping him remember the story, it likely will not allow him to maintain this skill.

15. A: Although each student is different and may require different levels of support, modifying the curriculum to allow the student to complete less work still allows the student to access the curriculum. Answer B is incorrect because completing work outside of the classroom does not allow him access to the teacher for instruction. Answers C and D are incorrect because just being in the classroom and not completing all of the required work does not allow a student to demonstrate knowledge of the curriculum.

16. D: Hesitating to contact a student's family because of the community that they live in is an example of a cultural bias. Being unfamiliar with a student's community should not necessarily be a reason to hesitate contacting the family. It is important to get to know students, but it is also important to understand that there are going to be some cultural differences between the student and teacher. Answer A is incorrect because simply having a negative encounter in the past does not necessarily mean that there is a cultural bias. Answer B is incorrect because not knowing the family history does not mean there is a bias; it simply means that the teacher is uninformed. Answer C is incorrect because an experience with the student's sibling does not necessarily indicate that there is a bias toward that culture.

17. A: The field of education is constantly changing; the same is true of policies and regulations pertaining to children with special needs. Teachers are usually the first people to identify or intervene when a child is struggling in class. All teachers should be responsible for educating themselves regarding possible problems that children might face. Without knowledge of symptoms, it will be impossible for a teacher to guide the student or parents effectively. The teacher may also find that previous knowledge of typical classroom strategies may benefit the child in question more quickly and may prevent problems from getting worse.

18. D: Assigning one student to compile and present the group's work could result in that student doing more of the project than the others. This would not be truly collaborative, so option A is incorrect.

Allowing students to volunteer to contribute to the project will result in some students doing most or all of the work while others end up doing little or none. This is not collaboration, so option B is incorrect.

The teacher leading the activity and directing what the students do would not be a collaborative group project. The students should be learning to cooperate with one another and to be more independent in conducting the project. The description in this option is a traditional teacher-led activity, so option C is incorrect.

Assigning each student an equal number of duties related to the project is a way to ensure that they all do equal amounts of work. The students will still be conducting the project themselves and working cooperatively together, but the teacher's initial assignment will prevent unequal distribution of participation, so option D is correct.

19. D: The audiologist is likely to deliver services to the hearing-impaired students. The SLP is likely to deliver services to both the students with hearing impairments and those with Down syndrome. The O&M specialist is likely to serve the visually impaired student. The OT is likely to serve the intellectually disabled and/or any students with poor fine motor control, common in this population. A PT would serve students with poor gross motor control, which is not identified here. Excluding testing as specified, a school psychologist and behavior specialist are less likely to serve this group, as no emotional, social, or behavioral problems are identified.

20. B: Cathy cannot communicate orally with caregivers due to her deafness. She is also less likely to initiate social interactions with caregivers due to her autism. Rather than serving no purpose (A), the self-injurious behavior she exhibits when in physical distress serves the purpose of attempting to communicate her distress and need for the relief caregivers can provide. Her coexisting conditions make this behavior more likely; however, the behavior is not caused by any one of them, (C) or (D).

21. D: Under IDEA, students with disabilities must be educated in the least restrictive environment, meaning they should be placed with nondisabled peers to the maximum extent appropriate. Removing this student from the general education setting for all classes when he only struggles in English violates LRE, because he could remain with his peers for subjects in which he is performing adequately while receiving targeted support for reading and writing.

22. D: Of all persons with learning disabilities, 80 percent (D) have reading disorders, making this the most common of the learning disabilities.

23. A: It is not true that the universal design (UD) approach (a) can only benefit LD students with the required adaptations. Adaptations are needed for some disabilities, but according to Ron Mace at the National Center for Universal Design at North Carolina State University, "Universal design is the design of products and environments to be usable by all people, to the greatest extent possible, without the need for adaptation or specialized design." UD does provide various methods of presenting content (b), so LD students unable to use one method can find another one more suited to their strengths. UD affords teachers more flexibility in the instructional strategies (c) they use, so they can select those more accessible and beneficial to individual LD students. UD also allows LD students different ways of demonstrating their mastery of content (d) so that disabilities in some forms of expression do not stop them from showing in other ways what they have learned.

24. C: The physical environment of a classroom is very important to effective learning. Classrooms that are bare will promote a cold, institutional feeling. This may inhibit learning. On the other hand, classrooms cluttered with information and posters may be too overwhelming for students and thus be counterproductive. In addition to ensuring that posters with appropriate content and an appropriate amount of information are used to decorate a room, proper lighting is also essential for creating an effective learning environment. Adequate lighting should be used to maintain attention and to prevent a dark environment where students and the teacher become sleepy during the day. This is especially important after lunch. If a classroom does not have enough lighting, the teacher can use lamps to increase the brightness of a room.

25. B: Although standardized tests are merely the result of one assessment, they tend to be a good indication of students' academic performance capabilities. Statewide tests are usually well constructed as the tests are analyzed and refined for significance over time. It is likely that the student is not giving as much effort in other areas if the results were significantly higher. Oftentimes, lower performance on homework and classwork is a result of boredom or distractions, and the teacher should respond by investigating what the source of the low scores is. It is also unreasonable to assume that the standardized test is not age appropriate when other students are performing as expected on the test.

26. B: A child that is between the ages of 2 and 6 will typically start to use perception in their thought process. Children at this age tend to be able to solve simple problems rather than complex, multidimensional ones. Psychologist Jean Piaget proposed that a child's intellectual development progresses through four stages. Answer A is incorrect because a child that is manipulating objects would typically be younger than 2. Answer C is incorrect because a child that applies logical reasoning will likely be older than 7. Answer D is incorrect because a child that has abstract thoughts will likely be 12 or older.

27. A: According to Piaget, elementary-school-age children are in the stage of concrete operations. They can understand mental operations and their reversibility for the first time. Piaget said that children develop certain conservation skills earlier and others later. Conservation of number develops earliest, usually around ages five to seven years. The children in this question have mild developmental delays. So it can be expected that some of them may have developed this understanding and some have not. This would be a good task to offer them at their age. Therefore, option A is correct.

Class inclusion is typically acquired around the age of seven or eight. These children are only six and also have mild developmental delays, so they may be a year or two behind other children in cognitive development. In tests with the 20-questions game, children six to eight with normal cognitive development would simply guess (e.g., "Is it a banana?"), whereas children aged nine to eleven would think in terms of categories (e.g., "Is it something you eat?"), showing the ability of classification. A class inclusion task for six-year-olds with mild developmental delays would be too advanced, and they would probably all fail at it. Therefore, option B is incorrect.

Conservation of weight usually develops around the ages of nine to ten. This would be beyond the development of cognitively average six-year-olds, let alone those with mild developmental delays. Therefore, option C is incorrect.

Conservation of volume is typically attained around the ages of twelve to fourteen, according to Piaget. It would be far beyond the cognitive abilities of six-year-olds. Therefore, option D is incorrect.

28. A: For a functional skills assessment for a secondary school student with an intellectual disability, you should obtain (A) a vocational skills assessment because the student is nearing the age when he or she may need to work. You would not obtain IQ test results (B) for a *functional* skills assessment because IQ shows intellectual rather than functional skills. Tests of motor development (C) are more appropriate for younger children who are still developing and could be developing slower than the norm. By high school age, a student without physical disabilities does not have as much motor development yet to undergo as a young child. SAT scores (D) can predict a student's ability to perform in higher educational settings but do not test skills for functioning in a job.

29. A: By the age of six, typical language development will include speaking in sentences of about five or six words. By this age, children tend to have a vocabulary of 2,000 or more words, so answer choice B is incorrect. Children at age six are also expected to communicate their age orally rather than with their fingers, so answer choice C is incorrect. They also no longer say simple phrases such as "me want," which eliminates answer choice D.

30. A: Although all these choices certainly have an impact, it is best that the students are grouped by ability level. Each student will have different IEP goals and progress toward those goals, so it is important to place students in groups that will allow for this progress. It may be difficult for students to make progress on these goals if they are in small groups in which they are not working at an appropriate instructional level. Answer B is incorrect because grouping students on their grade level may not help them make progress on their IEP goals because students might be at various skill levels. Answer C is incorrect because simply grouping students based on their teachers also may involve grouping students at various ability levels. Answer D is incorrect because although grouping students based on maturity level might be important, some students with similar maturity levels function at different academic levels.

31. D: Although all of these choices can be instrumental in establishing a safe classroom, building and maintaining relationships is the best long-term strategy for maintaining a safe classroom environment. When students feel important and there is a sense of trust with the teacher, the students will feel safer. If students do not have someone they can rely on, they will have a difficult time feeling safe. Answer A is incorrect because simply showing students where the exits are might not make them feel safe all the time. Answer B is incorrect because having a clean and orderly classroom is important, but it may not mean as much if the students do not feel valued. Answer C is incorrect because having the rules posted on the wall does not build a connection with the student that might make them feel safe.

32. C: A typical four-year-old would be expected to start cutting paper with scissors. This is an example of a fine motor skill because it is a skill that uses small muscles such as those of the hands and fingers rather than large muscles. It is important to recognize the difference between fine and gross motor skills in order to determine which may be age appropriate or could potentially be a deficit. Answer A is incorrect because hopping on one foot uses larger muscles groups so it would be an example of gross motor skills. Answer B is incorrect because catching a ball also would be considered an example of gross motor skills. Answer D is incorrect because riding a tricycle also involves the larger muscle groups in the legs.

33. C: Although it could be beneficial to conduct a verbal intelligence test on all these students, it would be most appropriate for a student with a writing disability. Students who struggle with communication, including writing, often struggle to express themselves. The verbal intelligence test measures this in order to determine if there are supports that can be put in place for students with these deficits. Answer A is incorrect because students with intellectual disabilities could struggle with these kinds of assessments, and other assessments would be more appropriate for reevaluating special education services. Answer B is incorrect because although students with math deficiencies may struggle with verbal intelligence, students who struggle with reading and writing are more likely to benefit from these tests. Answer D is incorrect because students with visual impairments will likely have a separate kind of assessment to measure their abilities in this area when reevaluating for special education services.

34. A: An ORF is an Oral Reading Fluency assessment. An ORF is a one-minute assessment in which the student reads a grade-level text aloud. The test supervisor notes errors that the reader doesn't self-correct and the number of words read correctly.

35. A: While all of these strategies could be helpful, maintaining consistency in the schedule is the foundational strategy for supporting students who have difficulty coping with change. When visitors or special events do occur, it helps, of course, to prepare the students by telling them in advance of the change in schedule. Those children who are still disturbed by the change can be helped by being near someone they trust during the visit or activity. The teacher can even teach relaxation techniques to the students and suggest these techniques when a student appears to be having anxiety over a change in routine, but these strategies are secondary to maintaining the schedule as much as possible.

36. D: For students who are learning about life skills, the practical application portion of the lesson is most important for them to practice their skills. Answer A is incorrect; although it is important for them to know the objective, the application tends to be more productive and memorable. Similarly, while warmups may be useful, they are less important than the practical application portion of a life skills class. Therefore, answer B is incorrect. Answer C is incorrect because life skills are often easier learned by doing rather than lectures.

37. C: Although all of these choices may impact students throughout their lifetimes, students with multiple disabilities are likely to be impacted the most. Students with multiple disabilities have two or more disabilities that severely impact their access to education. One of these disabilities is typically an intellectual disability, which impacts students throughout their life. Answer A is incorrect because developmental delays typically impact younger students and may or may not last throughout a person's lifetime. Answer B is incorrect because students that have just speech or language impairments may end up learning to overcome these disabilities eventually. Answer D is incorrect because although specific learning disabilities may impact students in different ways, these are less likely to have an impact on a person than someone with multiple disabilities.

38. A: When assessing a student for fine motor skills, it is important to take a look at activities such as drawing, writing, and using scissors. These kinds of skills are considered fine movements in that they are smaller movements that involve the hands, wrists, fingers, or toes. These kinds of assessments are important for determining whether or not a student needs additional support with a skill such as handwriting. Answer B is incorrect because while watching a student making numbers with their hands can be a form of fine motor assessment, it is not as relevant to the fine motor skills needed in a classroom setting as drawing a picture would be. Answer C is incorrect because watching a student throw a ball would be looking at gross motor abilities. Answer D is incorrect because watching a student riding a bike would also be looking at gross motor skills.

39. B: The calculator is considered mid tech because it is an example of a device that requires technology but does not typically need to be plugged in or require much maintenance. Calculators are typically used for students who struggle with math calculations and require extra support in the classroom. This kind of assistive technology can be beneficial in that it does not require much more than carrying the calculator to class. Answer a is incorrect because low-tech assistive devices would include everyday items such as pencil grips and graphic organizers. Answer c is incorrect because high-tech assistive devices would include devices that require more maintenance including text-to-speech software and tablets. Answer d is incorrect because no-tech options typically refer to instructional or environmental strategies that do not involve specialized equipment, whereas a calculator is a device that helps a student access the curriculum and is categorized as mid-tech assistive technology.

40. A: In order for students to be able to generalize a skill or concept, it is important for them to practice it across various settings. Practicing name writing inside the same classroom where it was taught does not generalize this skill. It is also important to not only practice in different settings but also with assistance from a variety of people. Answer B is incorrect because practicing at home with their parents can be an effective way to generalize this skill. Answer C is incorrect because practicing in art class gives them a new environment in which to work on the same skills. Answer D is incorrect because practicing with friends can also be beneficial in generalizing the skill.

41. A: Cooperative learning can be beneficial to students with all kinds of disabilities because it allows for smaller groups to work together. Rather than the teacher doing the majority of instructing, cooperative learning allows the students to work together to solve problems. Many students with disabilities may struggle to participate in large class discussions, but this gives them a different kind of opportunity to learn. Answer B is incorrect because there is likely going to be the same level of support in these classes. Answer C is incorrect because students tend to receive less direct instruction from teachers in cooperative learning classrooms. Answer D is incorrect because students may or may not make more progress on IEP goals depending on the student and the goals.

42. D: Students with learning disabilities often avoid asking questions in large classes/groups. Teachers can encourage them to take risks by giving cues that support their asking "wh-" questions.

Pairing students to discuss teacher questions (A) is a good strategy to engage all LD students in a large class. Asking LD students to summarize main lesson points (B) is a good strategy to discern whether they understand these, and reviewing benefits all students. Having LD students complete reminder worksheets at the end of the lesson (C) is a good strategy to see what they have learned, what they enjoyed, and what else they know about the subject.

43. D: All students can benefit from movement activities as a method of stimulating their brain, so incorporating this strategy for all students would be the most beneficial. Although it may not always be possible each class period, finding creative ways to get Zachary up and moving with the rest of the class will make him feel less singled out. It is important to develop a plan for when these movement breaks are needed for students like Zachary and how they can be implemented for the entire class. Answer A is incorrect because Zachary may take advantage of the pass system and use it more than he really needs to. Answer B is incorrect because giving him a timer also might become a distraction to Zachary and other students around him. Answer C is incorrect because giving a student his own area might end up making him feel singled out.

44. A: Giving into peer pressure represents conformity, which means changing one's behavior to be more like the norm. This can have both negative and positive effects. Negative effects include a loss of individual identity and a potential to engage in dangerous behaviors. Positive effects include social acceptance and greater group cohesion. Independence and individualism are the result of thinking for oneself. While someone could feel guilt for giving into peer pressure, this is not always true.

45. A: A classroom with rows of desks allows the support personnel to move up and down the aisles to support students. It is important that students that require support have access to that support person, who can help them if needed. Answer B is incorrect because having clusters of desks may make it difficult to access individual students. Answer C is incorrect because having desks in circles may also make it difficult to work with students. Answer D is incorrect because having long tables also limits this access.

46. D: Although all of these choices may be beneficial for students with autism, providing hands-on instruction would likely be the best option. It is important to provide different options for students to learn, especially those students who may struggle with the content. Giving students an opportunity to learn and demonstrate their knowledge using their hands can help them to retain the information. Answers A and C are incorrect because although cross-curricular connections and choices can be effective supports, they are less directly targeted to math concept acquisition than hands-on work in this context. Answer B is incorrect because giving a student multiple tasks might be difficult if they are struggling with the first task.

47. C: Between the ages of 3 and 5 years old, the vocabulary of a child expands considerably, sometimes even more than doubling. The other options list milestones that generally occur at later stages in a child's development.

48. B: Often, children have richer vocabularies than they realize. This project simultaneously encourages students to remember words they already know and to learn other words with similar meanings from the world around them.

49. A: A score of 100 on a standard IQ test indicates a score that is right in the middle of the average range when compared to other students his age. This indicates that Ricky's intelligence is where it is expected to be for someone his age. Additional assessments are necessary to determine whether he does or does not need special education services, however. Answer B is incorrect because a score of 100 is in the middle of the data, not an indication that he scored 100% on the test. Answer C is incorrect because additional assessments must be conducted to determine his need for services. Answer D is incorrect because Ricky may not need services, depending on the results of other assessments.

50. D: Although all these choices may be beneficial for students who struggle with reading comprehension, using a tablet allows the student to practice reading and answering questions. It is important for students to practice these skills as much as possible in order to improve them. For many students, using a tablet to read a story may yield better results than simply reading the story and taking a quiz or test. Answer A is incorrect because although audiobooks can be a useful accommodation, it would likely be more productive to have students practice the skill of reading independently when focusing on reading comprehension. Answer B is incorrect because although this may be helpful for students, practicing their comprehension skills is likely a better strategy. Answer C is incorrect because speech-to-text software would be more effective for students who struggle with writing.

51. C: Although there are many uses for intelligence tests, determining which accommodations a student accesses can help guide instruction. Intelligence testing is important in determining the intellectual abilities of students. These results can reveal how accommodations may benefit them in the classroom and which ones would be the most appropriate for them to access. Answer A is incorrect because although an intelligence test can be helpful in determining whether or not a student has an intellectual disability, this does not alone determine whether a student qualifies for special education services. Answer B is incorrect because determining whether a student has an emotional disability would likely encompass more than just an intelligence test. Answer D is incorrect because learning disabilities are typically discovered through additional assessments as well.

52. D: T stands for Time-based, i.e., the objective should specify in what length of time, or by what point in time, it is to be attained. M stands not for Memorable (A), but Measurable: the objective must be something that can be objectively measured or quantified. A stands not for Activities (B), but Appropriate: the objective should be suitable to the purpose the activity is intended to accomplish. R stands not for Resources (C), but Realistic: the objective should be possible to achieve with the instructional experience and resources available.

53. A: Although all these strategies can be beneficial in overcoming cultural biases, learning why the bias occurs is likely to be the most effective. If teachers are able to analyze and understand why some of the biases occur, they may be able to eliminate them or overcome them. Cultural biases occur for many reasons, but it is important to understand the impact that a teacher has and what the needs of the student might be. Answer B is incorrect because being objective may not be quite as effective as showing empathy for certain students. Answer C is incorrect because not all students will likely learn the same way, so they should not necessarily be treated the same. Answer D is incorrect because simply encouraging these cross-group interactions may or may not help in overcoming personal biases.

54. A: In order for a student like Jessica to succeed in the general education setting, it is likely best to differentiate the learning environment. One way to do this would be to create a space in the classroom where there are no distractions. This way, Jessica can still access the content of her peers while being free from distractions that might impact her ability to learn. Answer B is incorrect because differentiating the content would not be appropriate; she can still learn what the other students learn. Answer C is incorrect because differentiating the process would not be appropriate; she can still learn the content in the same way that the other students learn. Answer D is incorrect because differentiating the product would not be appropriate; she can be assessed using the same methods as other students.

55. B: When teaching students with coexisting disabilities, it is important to look at the student as a whole rather than someone with more than one disability. It is difficult to meet each and every need of the student if he or she is looked at separately. It is important to look at the student as a whole and discover how his or her needs can be met.

56. C: Although some parents are difficult to contact and do not wish to be involved with their child's education, providing alternatives might be the best option. It is important to accommodate the needs of the parents whenever possible in an attempt to get them more involved. The input of the parents is very valuable at IEP meetings, so if having them participate by phone is the best option for them, then that should be explored. Answer A is incorrect because they are unlikely to respond if they continue to receive phone calls nonstop. Answer B is incorrect because although sending forms home may work for some parents, some kind of verbal communication would likely be more productive. Answer D is incorrect because it is important to have input from the family members that live with the student.

57. D: Although all of these choices may benefit Corey to a certain extent, providing one-to-one intervention in reading fluency is most likely to improve his reading fluency. One-to-one instruction allows Corey to move at his own pace and move on to the next skill when he has mastered the previous skill. This allows the teacher to truly meet Corey's needs in reading fluency and give him complete attention during the intervention time. Answer A is incorrect because a student with a severe deficiency in reading fluency likely needs additional intervention outside the classroom. Answer B is incorrect because a small group would not allow Corey to work at his own pace and provide the individual instruction that he may need. Answer C is incorrect because modifying the material will not allow Corey to build his reading fluency skills.

58. A: James can grasp an object inserted into his fist, so he could point to various pictures on a communication board with a pointer to communicate his needs. Therefore, option A is correct.

A computer with keyboard would not help James. He does not have the manual ability to type due to his contractures. He is also illiterate. Therefore, option B is incorrect.

A voice-activated computer would not do any good as James cannot speak. Therefore, option C is incorrect.

An adaptive holder for manipulating a pen would not work for James, as he could not use it due to the severe contractures of his hands, and he cannot read or write. Therefore, option D is incorrect.

59. B: It is an informal assessment of their writing and also gives the teacher an idea of each student's interests, abilities, and skills. This assignment gives the teacher an idea of her students' writing abilities at the beginning of the year. She can return to this piece of writing during the school year to assess progress.

60. D: When assessing students at the end of a unit who are working on executive functioning skills, it is best to see what they are able to do. A performance task allows them to complete a task that demonstrates their knowledge of executive functioning and explicitly targets planning, organization, time management, etc. Answer A is incorrect because a test doesn't show that they can complete a certain task. Answer B is incorrect because an essay would not show that they can perform certain skills they may have learned. Answer C is incorrect because presenting information does not necessarily mean that they have learned to complete something on their own.

61. A: One general problem that elementary school teachers face when teaching culturally diverse students is that most textbooks introduce a large number of new concepts to be taught within a short time frame. Another problem is that many of these texts' teacher editions do not offer tips for meeting the needs of culturally diverse students (B). An additional problem is that the reading levels of most texts are too difficult for many diverse students (C). As a result, teachers must differentiate their instruction for diverse students in general education classrooms because the books they use will not preclude this need (D).

62. B: For teachers who like to use a lot of discussion in their class, one strategy is to have the desks facing each other. This allows the students to communicate directly to each other and have conversations rather than the teacher doing most of the talking. This can also allow everyone in the class, including students with disabilities, to feel needed and included in the group. Answer A is incorrect because most classrooms likely do not have enough space to accommodate a meeting area large enough for multiple students. Additionally, a meeting area would not support on-going classroom discussion throughout the day in the same way that having desks always facing each other would. Answer C is incorrect because although having tables might be helpful, it may be difficult for students to communicate with everyone in the class when they are at a table. Answer D is incorrect because although ensuring that students can move around is beneficial, it is more important that they can communicate with each other.

63. D: Students with disabilities often suffer from learned helplessness, or a condition in which they feel like they have no control. These students will often give up because they think that nothing can be done to improve their condition. This is something that impacts individuals with disabilities as they are learning about themselves and what they are able to accomplish. Answer A is incorrect because students with disabilities will often suffer from learned helplessness. Answer B is incorrect because these students with learned helplessness have a difficult time controlling situations. Answer C is incorrect because students with disabilities do not always have the chance to reach out for help before they get to learned helplessness.

64. B: A maze test is a specific type of cloze test. In a cloze test, words are deleted, and the reader must supply the missing words using contextual clues and vocabulary that is familiar. A maze test is essentially a multiple-choice application of a cloze test.

65. A: Although all of these choices may be the responsibility for special education teachers some of the time, monitoring the progress of his goals will always be the responsibility of the special education teacher. Students with learning disabilities will have academic goals that the special education teacher will need to monitor frequently. It is important for the special education teacher to monitor the goals of students to ensure that progress is being made and decide if new interventions need to be put into place. Answer B is incorrect because providing mental health support is not likely to be the responsibility of the special education teacher. Answer C is incorrect because students with learning disabilities do not always have modifications; this depends on impact of their disability. Answer D is incorrect because students with learning disabilities may or may not need to access executive functioning support.

66. C: Students in elementary school do not typically attend their IEP meetings. These students are often too young to attend and understand the discussion at the meeting, so they are most often not invited to the meeting. It is important to understand a student's maturity level before inviting him or her to an important meeting to discuss the IEP. Answer A is incorrect because the school psychologist can be an important member of the IEP team for students with emotional disturbances in writing behavior plans or monitoring goals. Answer B is incorrect because the director of special education is also often invited to these IEP meetings. Answer D is incorrect because most school districts require a building administrator to attend IEP meetings as well.

67. A: Students who are eligible to take alternate assessment due to the impact of their disability will likely not take the same standardized tests as their peers. These students will likely struggle with the standardized test, and the alternate assessment will provide more valuable information. Answer B is incorrect because students new to the school can still take standardized tests, as they are the same for every grade level. Answer C is incorrect; although students with absences may struggle more with the test, it is still valuable in determining what they know. Answer D is incorrect because students with accommodations can access those for standardized tests.

68. D: When lesson planning, a warm-up is beneficial in that it provides students an opportunity to practice some of the skills they are going to learn in that lesson, which is connected to previous knowledge. To learn how to add and subtract fractions, it would be beneficial to practice adding and subtracting whole numbers. Answer A is incorrect because multiplying and dividing fractions is typically more advanced than adding and subtracting fractions, and Answer B is incorrect because a warm-up should review prerequisite skills rather than ask students to perform the new skill before it is taught. Answer C may be a good warm-up, but it is best practice for the warmup to relate directly to the lesson, so answer D is the best option.

69. C: Shirley's program should be re-evaluated because her objective criterion is 90%, but she has scored 75% for four tests in a row. It is not valid to assume she may be unable to reach 90% (A) because she already reached 90% once (point 3). While her last four scores were consistent, they cannot be considered successful (B) because they do not meet the objective criterion. It cannot be assumed she simply needs more time (D), because her scores initially improved but then fell and have not changed over four tests. Her program should be adjusted to enable her to progress to and maintain 90%.

70. C: Although all of these grouping patterns have their own strengths and weaknesses, it makes the least sense to group students based on their disability. It is important to take into consideration many aspects including disability, but this is unlikely to be the determining factor. It is more important that the students in the group are a good match for the instruction and each other than what their disability might be. Answer A is incorrect because grouping students by ability can be effective in ensuring that the students learn at a similar pace. Answer B is incorrect because grouping by age can help ensure the students are learning the same content in class. Answer D is incorrect because grouping students by behavior can help make sure that students work well with each other.

71. B: Since he is blind, Bert could not read a printed or written worksheet or circle and cross out word pairs. Therefore, option A is incorrect.

Both students could listen to word pairs read aloud. Even with poor fine motor skills, Nan has the gross motor skills to raise her hands. Therefore, option B is correct.

As Nan has poor fine motor skills, she might have difficulty circling or crossing out words, especially since she is only in first grade. Therefore, option C is incorrect.

Having Nan read a list of word pairs aloud to Bert would give Bert but not Nan the opportunity to show recognition of rhymes. Therefore, option D is incorrect.

72. D: In this example, Mr. Law is teaching his students word analysis by showing them how to break a complex word down into its prefixes, root words, and suffixes. Knowing these facilitates deducing the meaning of a word by knowing the meanings of each or some of the word's parts. Multiple exposures (A) would involve his presenting this same word to the class in repeated instances and a variety of contexts. Choosing appropriate words (B) would involve his making deliberate word choices that are congruent with his subject and level of instruction. Making a contextual analysis (C) would involve his asking the students to deduce the meaning of a word by finding clues in the sentence and/or the paragraph surrounding it.

73. B: When changing the environment and providing reinforcement systems, (B) the measures taken should vary according to the intensity of each individual student's behaviors. Behavior management strategies for students with emotional or behavioral disturbances should be individualized. They should not be the same for all students and behaviors (A). The favored approach is not always beginning with more intrusion and gradually decreasing it (C), but the opposite: beginning with the least intrusive intervention likely to work, and only increasing the intrusion level if necessary, i.e., less intrusive tactics, properly implemented, fail. Interventions should not always begin with more intensity and fade with progress (D). In fact, primary level interventions introduced early can prevent many later problems, as can secondary level interventions as needed. Waiting until a behavior escalates to the level of needing tertiary intervention can occur when this level is the only one that gets educators' attention, but this is too late to address the behavior optimally. Interventions should match the target behaviors in intensity. Earlier, less intense intervention when the behavior's intensity is milder is both easier to accomplish and more effective for prevention.

74. A: In order to assess a student for oral expression abilities, a test to measure their expressive language abilities is most appropriate. Students who struggle with oral expression tend to struggle expressing themselves orally due to many factors. This kind of assessment can guide the data collection needed for instruction in the classroom and skills to work on. Answer B is incorrect because receptive language assessments are more appropriate for students who struggle with language input rather than output. Answer C is incorrect because auditory discrimination tests are used for students who struggle with different sounds. Answer D is incorrect because this kind of assessment would be more appropriate in measuring a student's cognitive abilities.

75. D: Substance abuse can be an extremely detrimental environment factor, especially for those with mental health concerns. Substance abuse can either lead to mental health concerns in family members, or it can be a cause of concern in the student. It is important to understand some of the causes of the concerns that students are reporting in order to intervene as early as possible. Answer A is incorrect because although sleep deprivation can impact students with mental health concerns, it likely does not have the same impact as substance abuse. Answer B is incorrect because smoking is likely to have more of an impact on a person's physical health. Answer C is incorrect because although exposure to toxins can be detrimental to a person's health, it likely has more of an impact on physical health.

76. B: A student's IEP team does determine his/her eligibility for an alternate curriculum program. These programs are not the first choice for students with disabilities (A) and are not preferred over general curricula with accommodations and/or modifications (C). Rather, if an individual student still finds the general education curriculum too demanding even with accommodations and modifications provided, then an alternate curriculum program is a placement to consider. Students in these programs are typically assigned to a special education classroom as their primary placement but may also attend some general education classes and enrichment activities during the school day to interact with students without disabilities (D).

77. B: To supplement the curriculum for someone with Down syndrome, it is best to focus on skills that a student is likely to use for the rest of his or her life. Answer A is incorrect; although addition facts are important, being able to tell time is a skill that will need to be used every day. Answer C is incorrect because measuring is not a skill that a student with Down syndrome will likely use as much as time telling. Answer D is incorrect because using order of operations is a complex skill that is not functional.

78. C: The WISC and the WIAT (C) are most amenable to direct comparisons of ability and achievement. The WISC, or Wechsler Intelligence Scales for Children (WISC-IV), is for assessing intelligence with subscales for various dimensions (verbal, numerical, spatial, memory, etc.), while the WIAT, or Wechsler Individual Achievement Test, allows norm-referencing for the student's age/grade level. Both authored by David Wechsler and co-normed, they are thus most compatible for comparing intellectual ability with school achievement. The WRAT (Wide Range Achievement Test) (A and B), assesses reading recognition, spelling, and mathematical computation. It can identify error patterns to inform instructional plans, but it is not as easy to compare with the Wechsler IQ test as the Wechsler achievement test is. As answer choice C is correct, answer choice D, none of these, is incorrect.

79. A: According to IDEA, birth trauma would not be considered one of the causes of traumatic brain injury. Students with birth trauma would likely be considered under a different eligibility category. Students who receive services under the traumatic brain injury category will typically have a medical diagnosis of a traumatic brain injury. Answer B is incorrect because combat injuries can be one of the causes of traumatic brain injuries, even at a young age. Answer C is incorrect because violence is often associated with students who are impacted by traumatic brain injuries. Answer D is incorrect because sports-related injuries can also cause damage to the brain and cause traumatic brain injuries.

80. C: Because students learn in different ways, it is important to incorporate differentiated instruction in order to create the best learning environment for all students. This involves providing choice and changing content, product, process, or environment based on student needs. Choice C gives students the option to choose a project format that works best for them, so it is an example of differentiated instruction. Options A and B are undifferentiated, as they provide the same content in the same way to all students. While choice D could be beneficial in expressing diversity and connecting with students of various nationalities, it also provides the same content in the same manner to all students.